The Global Challenge to Industrial Districts

The Global Challenge to Industrial Districts

Small and Medium-sized Enterprises in Italy and Taiwan

Edited by

Paolo Guerrieri

Simona Iammarino

Carlo Pietrobelli

Edward Elgar

Cheltenham, UK • Northampton, MA, USA

Published by
Edward Elgar Publishing Limited
Glensanda House
Montpellier Parade
Cheltenham
Glos GL50 1UA
UK

Edward Elgar Publishing, Inc.
136 West Street
Suite 202
Northampton
Massachusetts 01060
USA

A catalogue record for this book
is available from the British Library

Library of Congress Cataloguing in Publication Data

The global challenge to industrial districts : small and medium sized enterprises in Italy and Taiwan / edited by Paolo Guerrieri, Simona Iammarino, Carlo Pietrobelli.
    p. cm.
    Includes bibliographical references and index.
    1. Industrial districts—Italy. 2. Industrial districts—Taiwan.
3. Competition, International. 4. Globalization—Economic aspects.
I. Guerrieri, Paolo, 1947– II. Iammarino, Simona III. Pietrobelli, Carlo, 1959–

HC310.D5 G56 2001
338.6'42'0945—dc21

                                                                2001033071

ISBN 1 84064 698 5 (cased)
Printed and bound in Great Britain by Biddles Ltd, *www.biddles.co.uk*

Contents

Figures

Tables

Contributors

Dieter Ernst is Professor of Economics at the East-West Center, Honolulu, Hawaii,USA.

Paolo Guerrieri is Professor of International Economics at the University of Rome, La Sapienza, Italy, and at the College of Europe, Bruges, Belgium, and Senior Fellow at the Institute for International Affairs (IAI), Rome, Italy

Simona Iammarino is Research Fellow at the Italian National Institute of Statistics (ISTAT) and Senior Fellow in Economics at the Institute for International Affairs (IAI), Rome, Italy.

Wen-Jeng Kuo was Research Fellow at the Chung-Hua Institution for Economic Research, Taipei, Taiwan, and he is now an independent consultant.

Carlo Pietrobelli is Professor of Development Economics at the University of Molise, Campobasso, Italy, and Senior Fellow in Economics at the Institute for International Affairs (IAI), Rome, Italy, and at CEIS, University of Rome, Tor Vergata.

Jiann-Chyuan Wang is Research Fellow at the Chung-Hua Institution for Economic Research, Taipei, Taiwan.

Foreword

John Cantwell

Much of the literature on industrial districts and on local areas as centres for innovation suffers from the defect that it focuses almost entirely on the interchanges that occur within such areas between small and medium-sized enterprises (SMEs). This literature has rarely paid much attention to the role of larger leader companies within such localities, or to the connections with complementary innovation in other distant sites that is provided when these larger firms are part of a multinational corporation (MNC). This book is welcome both because it begins to redress the balance by considering MNCs and Global Production Networks (GPN), and particularly because it does so in the context of a systematic international comparison, distinguishing between the experience of Italy (in Europe) and Taiwan (in East Asia). Besides the empirical evidence that it provides on the restructuring of competitiveness in different types of industrial clusters, the authors have used their assessment of this evidence to give us some helpful new conceptualizations of the issues involved in localized innovation systems in a globalised environment.

In some earlier work that Simona Iammarino and I had done on innovation by foreign-owned MNCs in the European regions, we had distinguished between major centres of innovative activity or 'higher order' regions, smaller more specialized centres or 'intermediate' regions, and areas to which little innovative capacity is attracted or 'lower order' regions. These areas differ both with respect to the type and extent of MNC activity that they attract, and with respect to the impact of MNCs on other firms in the locations in which they invest. In general terms, MNCs are more likely to site research-intensive technologically advanced production in higher order regions, while lower order regions tend to attract mainly just the assembly-type of operations of MNCs. What is more, while MNC affiliates in intermediate regions tend to tap into the specific fields of local technological specialization (and so their effect is to deepen established specialization and to involve mainly intra-industry inter-firm networks), in higher order centres MNCs often develop general purpose technologies which are multi-purpose and not industry-specific (and so their effect is to widen local specialization and to offer the potential of inter-industry inter-company networks).

Thus, when considering the effects of cross-border MNC development on smaller and more localized (non-multinational) firms, the kinds of spillovers which occur between firms within clusters are likely to differ according to the position of the local system in a geographical hierarchy and to the prevailing pattern of local agglomeration of sectoral activities (that is, the industrial district in Italy, the county-district in Taiwan). For example, in intermediate regions technology spillovers are typically intra-industry or at least involve a common set of broad technological fields, and hence reinforce the established pattern of specialization (such as within motor vehicle and related engineering in Piemonte). Conversely, in higher order regions spillovers occur much more in fields of technology that are common to many industries, such as in general mechanical processes, information and communication technologies, or new materials, and the existence of these kinds of localized network externalities increases the attractiveness of such areas for foreign-owned corporate technological development in general. The availability of localized technology spillovers within regions in turn increases the potential for foreign-owned affiliates to acquire an independently technologically creative role within their international corporate groups, to which they are connected (among other things) by means of cross-border knowledge flows.

For all the different geographical clusters in which some significant MNC activity is located, as in the case of Taiwan, international networks provide a linkage mechanism for all local companies - including SMEs - to innovation in other geographically distant regions, which allows each area to become more specialized in the fields of its own greatest potential, while better appreciating and responding to complementary technological development elsewhere in the world (mainly elsewhere in Europe in the Italian case, and elsewhere in East Asia in the Taiwanese case). Hence, the growing intensity of cross-border knowledge flows in each economy (whether in the context of the EU or of ASEAN) and the emergence of a new kind of relationship between economic activities and space help to promote and not to hinder innovative efforts, with respect to both flows between firms (often within regions) and between regions (often within MNCs).

This book goes further by taking down to a more micro-geographical level a related analysis of innovation in the location and the firm, with specific reference to the role of both the SME and the MNC. It shares this perspective that both localized and international knowledge exchanges are important and that the coevolution of interactions between local systems of SMEs (with their tacit and contextual knowledge) and the codified knowledge generated at the global level is a crucial factor for the future competitiveness, but it demonstrates just how and why they matter in the different settings of Italy and Taiwan. I am happy to encourage those that have an interest in these subjects to read further, and to explore the insights and the case details that you will find here.

Acknowledgements

The research leading to this volume has been supported by the European Commission through the DGXII TSER Project 'SMEs in Europe and East Asia: Competition, Collaboration and Lessons for Policy Support' (Contract No. SOE1CT97-1065). We would like to thank all the members of the European network involved in the project for the many useful discussions, Professor Martin Fransman for co-ordinating the project, and Professor Sanjaya Lall for his comments and support to organize and carry out the Taiwanese field study.

Preliminary versions of the various chapters were presented at the AISSEC XII Conference, Certosa di Pontignano (Siena), Italy, June 3-5, 1999, at the DRUID Summer Conference, Aalborg University, Denmark, June 15-17, 2000, at the *Universidad Nacional del Sur*, Bahía Blanca Argentina, February 2000, and at the International Workshop on Regional Growth, Clusters and Institutions, Stockholm, Sweden, June 19-20, 2000.

We would like to thank our Taiwanese partners, the Chung-Hua Institution for Economic Research in Taipei for the hospitality received, and particularly Dr Chaw-Hsia Tu for her active and precious collaboration during the project.

We also thank Federico Castellano, Felipe Diaz, Christina Franca Sousa and Tatiana Olarte Barrera for their skilful and enthusiastic research assistance.

Thanks also go to all our colleagues who participated in the debate, particularly those who acted as discussants in conferences and workshops, and the members of the European network involved in the project.

Paolo Guerrieri
Simona Iammarino
Carlo Pietrobelli

Rome, November 2000

Abbreviations

ASDL	Asymmetric Digital Subscriber Loop
BTO	Buy to order
COCOM	Co-ordinating Committee on Multilateral Export Controls
CPU	Central processing unit
CRT	Cathode ray tube
CS	Centre-Satellite Programme, Government of Taiwan
DRAM	Dynamic Random Access Memory
FDI	Foreign Direct Investment
GPN	Global production network
HP	Hewlett Packard
IC	Integrated circuits
ICT	Information and communication technology
ID	Industrial District
IECDF	International Economic Co-operation and Development Fund (Taiwan's foreign aid programme)
III	Institute for Information Industry, Taipei, Taiwan
IPO	International Procurement Office
ISDN	Integrated Services Digital Network
ITRI	Industrial Technology Research Institute
LANs	Local Area Networks
LCD	Liquid crystal display
MELCO	Mitsubishi Electric Corporation
MIC	Market Intelligence Centre
MNE	Multinational enterprise
MOEA	Ministry of Economic Affairs, Taiwan
NIE	Newly industrialized economy
NIT	New information technology
OBM	Original brand-name manufacturing
ODM	Original design manufacturing
OEM	Original equipment manufacturing
OPR	Overseas production ratio
PSTN	Public Switched Telephone Network
SME	Small and medium-sized enterprise
STN-LCD	Super-twist-nematic liquid crystal display

TFT	Thin-film-transistor
TI	Texas Instruments
TSMC	Taiwan Semiconductor Manufacturing Corporation
VCF	Venture Capital fund

Size:
Italy: 301,277 km^2
Taiwan: 35,980 km^2
Ratio: 8,4

1. Introduction

Paolo Guerrieri, Simona Iammarino and Carlo Pietrobelli

The central aim of this book is to analyse the relationship between the current globalization of economic and technological activities, and the strategy of firms with regard to geographical location and inter-firm linkage creation. The experience of small and medium-sized enterprises (SMEs) in Italy and Taiwan, where these enterprises substantially characterize the national industrial structure, offers an excellent and promising case to explore some aspects of such a crucial issue.

The internationalization of economic activities is changing the pattern of clustering and its rationale. In the context of global markets for goods, finance and technology, the agglomeration of economic activities matters for different reasons than in the past, and thereby must take a different form. Local sources of competitiveness are still crucial to obtain static and dynamic economies of scale and interactions for learning and innovation, while this needs to coexist with an opening to international markets to sell, as well as to source knowledge and technology world-wide. Furthermore, the relationship between the internationalization of markets and technology and the agglomeration of manufacturing and innovation is multifold and complex, as they may mutually reinforce each other and contribute to the acquisition of international competitiveness. In order to address this issue, we exploit the richness of two case studies on Italian and Taiwanese clusters of SMEs that have been carried out by means of direct interviews with a sample of SMEs in textiles and clothing, and in the electronic sector, in each country, respectively.

The comparisons that may be drawn from such analyses are insightful, as SMEs represent the bulk of industrial structures in both economies. For several decades Italy has represented the object of analysis of the theorists of clusters; and the notion of 'external economies' and Marshallian industrial districts have found their empirical illustration in this country. Moreover, and in contrast to other East-Asian economies, Taiwan's industry has also been largely dominated by SMEs.

Furthermore, both countries have been fully open to the

internationalization and globalization processes. Italy's performance in manufacturing exports, especially by SMEs, has been outstanding for many decades since the end of the Second World War and has managed to cope with the fiercer global competition of the most recent years. Taiwan has been one of the earliest developing countries to open to international economic flows, first targeting export markets, and then relying on the direct investments of foreign multinationals to foster its economic development. More recently, Taiwanese companies have also started to invest overseas and to strike strategic linkages (sometimes of an equity nature) with transnational corporations.

What makes the comparison especially instructive as well, is the countries' different pattern of industrial specialization. Italy has been, and still is, mainly specialized in 'traditional productions', sometimes the heritage of craftsmen's skills and capabilities developed over the centuries. The Italian export structure has been dominated by sectors such as furniture, textiles and clothing, ceramics, metalworking and industrial machines. The pattern of Italian foreign trade has hardly changed thereafter. In contrast, Taiwan, after an early phase of specialization in labour-intensive clothing, has been experiencing a steady and rapid diversification towards electronics and electrical machinery since the 1980s. Thus the structural transformation of the Taiwanese economy has been remarkable, and this has been reflected by the pattern of enterprise strategies and inter-firm linkages.

The globalization of technology and economic activities imposes changes and restructuring on the nature and organization of enterprise clusters. Agglomeration economies will continue to matter, but their strength and effects will increasingly depend upon the interaction with the global actors. This book will show why, and how, this is relevant for applied analyses of the evolution of industries, firms and clusters.

1. THE GLOBALIZATION OF ECONOMIC AND TECHNOLOGICAL ACTIVITIES

Globalization is one of the most widely used neologisms of this decade, and it has been applied to virtually every aspect of human life. A large amount of literature has focused on the globalization of technology, and this is not surprising (Archibugi and Michie, 1997). On the one hand, new technologies are a fundamental vehicle for the transmission of information and knowledge across different regions of the world. Information may be transferred from one part of the world to another at negligible costs thanks to the Internet, satellites and telecommunications, and this in turn has implications for the globalization of finance, production and culture. On the other hand, today, the production and diffusion of innovation is much more global in scope than in the past. Thus, regardless of the definitions and the classifications employed, and the indicators to measure it, the globalization of economic and technological activities has substantially risen during the last decade.[1]

Technology is increasingly exploited in international markets, and high-tech industries absorb more than one fifth of the world trade in manufacturing (Guerrieri, 1999). The extension of patents to foreign markets has also grown dramatically, suggesting that innovators have been attempting to exploit the results of innovation in overseas markets to a rising extent. The markets for seeking payoffs for investments in technology are becoming more and more global.

Technology is also being increasingly generated overseas, essentially through the activities of multinational enterprises (MNEs). A rising share of innovation of US and European MNEs is generated in foreign subsidiaries, and high-tech establishments operating in the USA today are also owned by non-US companies, a major change from the past; strategic technological collaborations and alliances are also increasingly international in scope (Hagedoorn, Link and Vonortas, 2000). This form of generating knowledge and technology has substantially increased its relevance and the number of recorded agreements has doubled over the last decade.

In sum, what we are observing is a major structural change that is having remarkable consequences on the functioning and organization of individual enterprises, as well as on entire economic systems. Undoubtedly, this is also bound to have remarkable implications for enterprise strategies, for the organization of production and of inter-firm relationships, and for the geography of economics and innovation.

2. THE CLUSTERING OF ECONOMIC ACTIVITIES: GEOGRAPHY MATTERS

There is a long tradition in industrial and regional economics, dating back to the 19th century, of explaining the tendency of industries to agglomerate in particular geographical locations (Guerrieri, Iammarino and Pietrobelli, 1998). Moreover, in the last few decades there has been a strong resurgence of interest in the economics of industrial location, following, on the one hand, the debates triggered by the 'new economic geography' (Krugman, 1991a, b) and, on the other hand, the insights of the heterodox approach to technological change proposed by the evolutionary theories (see, for example, Freeman, 1982; Nelson and Winter, 1982).

The phenomenon of the concentration of production in space, and its persistence over time, was first observed by Marshall (Marshall, 1891), who listed three fundamental advantages, in the form of externalities, for firms to locate in a cluster or a district:

1. a pooled market for skilled workers with industry-specific competencies, which, from the viewpoint of firms, prevents labour shortage;
2. the availability of non-tradable and intermediate inputs, provided by local suppliers;
3. the easy transmission of new ideas (knowledge and informational spillovers), which allow a better production function through technical, organizational and production improvements.

Both static and dynamic economies were thus identified by Marshall as one category of possible effects of the spatial agglomeration of economic activities, enhancing the efficiency and the growth of firms located in an industrial cluster.

For the sake of precision, a distinction is usually made between different types of agglomeration forces which shape spatial organization. On the one hand, there are general external economies and spillover effects (the so-called *urbanization economies*) which attract all kinds of economic activities in certain areas. This provokes the emergence of regional cores with sectoral specialization varying across different locations. On the other hand, *localization economies* are fostered in spatial clusters of firms undertaking related or similar activities. This kind of force is likely to be industry-specific and to produce cumulative mechanisms which enable host locations to increase their production, technological and organizational competence over time (Cantwell and Iammarino, 1998, 2001; Dicken and Lloyd, 1990). More generally, urbanization externalities arising between different industries can be essentially described as external economies resulting from the growth of the overall economic activity in a particular location; whilst location externalities are economies external to the firm but generated within the industry. However a real distinction is often difficult to establish, as in both cases economies of scale and scope originate from the efficiency and intensity of the linkages established among local actors, acting as barriers to entry for new firms, and locking in the initial advantage of the existing locations.

All these factors tend to determine cumulative mechanisms that may perpetuate the advantage of an area or a region over others. History and path-dependence play a specially important role in this context (Krugman, 1991b).

Most interesting to our aims is the causal relationship that several authors have suggested, and sometimes supported with empirical evidence, between geographical clustering and economic performance. In fact, innovation, as well as production, turns out to be spatially concentrated, and this can mainly be attributed to the benefits which stem from a specific form of agglomeration economies, that is, knowledge externalities (spillovers). Reference may once more be made to Marshall's work, suggesting that the accumulation of skills, know-how and knowledge, takes place within spatially bounded contexts, promoting a kind of 'industrial atmosphere' capable of enhancing economic growth. A dynamic interpretation of the concept of industrial district or system area is represented by the concept of 'milieu innovateur' (Capello, 1999), where dynamic synergies and collective learning explain innovation processes at the spatial level. The presence of a common knowledge which goes beyond the boundaries of the firm, but which remains within the spatial boundaries of the milieu, gives rise to a process of cumulative local know-how. Such processes of 'collective learning' positively affect innovation and knowledge creation.

Developing along the path set by the Marshallian tradition at the end of the 1970s, a group of Italian scholars introduced a new definition of industrial district, as 'a socio-territorial entity which is characterised by the active presence of both a community of people and a population of firms in one naturally and historically bounded area. In the district, unlike in other environments, such as manufacturing towns, community and firms tend to merge' (Becattini, 1990, p. 38). The distinctive factors of an industrial district appear to be: the concentration of production and innovative activities, both at the geographical and the sectoral level; the common social and cultural backgrounds; and the organization of linkages among business and non-business actors in formal and informal networks.

The remarkable *balance between competition and collaboration*, typically achieved in industrial districts, and the division of labour and specialization within the district, have led to a very successful performance on international markets for several decades.

3. GLOBALIZATION AND LOCALIZATION

Is the importance of geographical agglomeration bound to be inevitably wiped away by the rising and widespread globalization of economic and technological activities? The debate between the supporters of globalization and those arguing that agglomeration will remain a fundamental determinant of competitiveness, has been going on for a few years.

One extreme vision argues that globalization is, and will continue to be, the overall prevailing trend; the strongest force, sweeping away all other determinants of economic performance and organization (Ohmae, 1990). Such a 'techno-liberiste' vision is implicitly founded on the idea that knowledge and technology may be transferred geographically without any great difficulty, and that the innovative activity of enterprises has no need for the externalities produced by the public system. The obvious implication is that government policies to strengthen local technological competencies are irrelevant.

In contrast, other authors argue that taking into account the geographical dimension of globalization reveals a profound *interdependence between the global and the local*. Peter Dicken accurately emphasizes that 'global and local are not fixed scales; rather, they represent the extreme points of a dialectical continuum of complex mutual interactions' (Dicken, 1994, p. 103). Such interdependence has different implications for the various actors at stake, such as firms, states and regions.

Let us briefly explore the nexus between 'global' and 'local' for firms and MNEs. To the multinational firm, the global-local question with regard to production and innovative activities revolves mainly around the choice of location. This choice clearly depends upon both the strategy followed by the MNE, and the characteristics of the alternative local contexts where research and innovation may be located. Furthermore, from the perspective of the host region or country, globalization of the MNE's activities may improve local capabilities and strengthen the attractiveness of agglomeration (Cantwell and Iammarino, 2000, 2001). In order to exploit their competitive advantage, enterprises which relocate their production activities abroad may (under certain conditions) improve local productive capabilities by increasing the competitiveness of the recipient market and transferring technology and knowledge (Archibugi and Iammarino, 1998, Pietrobelli, 2000). From the point of view of the firm, therefore, the global-local nexus is driven by the aim to increase its global technological advantage from selected foreign sources (Cantwell, 1994). Traditional location advantages, that is, static endowments, are increasingly substituted by intangible assets such as localized accumulated knowledge and skills. Firms aim at creating or entering networks, generating a co-evolution of domestic and international knowledge linkages (Ernst, 1997).

More generally, competitive success depends on a firm's ability to manage inter-organizational knowledge creation. The generation of new capabilities is increasingly taking place through the combination of the capabilities of several firms and research organizations. The capability to selectively source specialized expertise outside the firm is crucial, and this requires a shift from individual to increasingly collective forms of organization that need to stretch out and reach distant global markets. This applies to innovation and technological capabilities, as well as to management capabilities, required to create and improve competitiveness.

Following the above considerations, there appears to be a fundamental interdependence between globalization and geographical agglomeration of economic activities and technology that is likely to hold even more in the future.

4. OPEN QUESTIONS AND ORGANIZATION OF THE BOOK

Several fundamental questions need to be posed at this stage: in which way will the trend towards globalization affect the type of advantages of clustering and geographical agglomeration? Firms' ability to achieve and sustain competitiveness seems increasingly to rely on their capacity to internationally relocate and disperse their production activities, or some stages of them, as well as to get integrated in global production and innovation networks. To what extent will the traditional advantages of geographical agglomeration play a role in what appears to be a 'global' economy?

More specifically, are Marshallian Industrial Districts (IDs), and particularly their Italian version, really less equipped to cope with the current structural, technological transformations and to provide a complex and articulated response? The strategy that has been frequently adopted in industrial districts, and that has often been very effective in fostering a remarkable export performance, has relied on deepening product specialization and improving product quality, marketing and distribution, thereby ensuring quick reaction to changes in market demand. Is this strategy going to be sufficient to exploit the new technological opportunities promising faster and more sustained demand in world markets?

Will different forms of organization of inter-firm relationships, such as hub-and-spoke variants of clustering (with one or more hubs or 'leaders') or 'global production networks' prove more efficient in facilitating the upgrading of the specialization pattern towards more technologically complex activities?

The theory of the evolution of enterprise clusters is explored in Chapter 2, in light of the peculiar features of technology and technological change. We shall notice how little attention has been paid to the transformation of clusters and to models geared to explaining their shift from one pattern of internal organization to another. This contrasts with the increasing evidence that clusters vary in size and stage of development on the one hand, and that they do reorganize and restructure in response to a changing environment of globalized economic and financial activities, on the other.

What implications does the shift of technological regime, within which firms operate, have upon enterprise clusters' internal organization, geographical location and innovative behaviour?

The prevailing techno-economic model, with the breaking through of the information and communication technologies (ICTs) and the rapid internationalization of all economic and technological activities, would seem to have diminished the traditional role of geographical location. But all this reveals only one side of the coin. In fact location remains fundamental to competition, albeit in different ways, in the new techno-economic model dominated by ICTs (Cox, 1997; Storper and Salais, 1997). The relevant knowledge base involves tacit as well as increasingly codified aspects. Indeed, if technology and equipment can be out-sourced, more advanced dimensions of competition remain geographically bounded. The enduring technological and competitive advantages in a global economy are often still significantly local.

In this perspective, the concept of a Global Production Network (GPN) has been indicated as one of the principal channels, especially for SMEs, to become integrated in the process of international knowledge creation, adoption and improvement (Chapter 5 in this volume). The spread of GPNs may be understood as an organizational innovation that may enable a firm to gain quick access to higher quality and/or lower cost foreign capabilities which are complementary to its own competencies, while maintaining an effective home base for innovation activities.

The empirical evidence in the Italian case is presented in Chapter 3, which provides some support to the hypothesis of different paths of ID dynamics according to the different capacities to react to global and technological challenges and the consequent restructuring of the ID competitiveness. Overall, the evidence seems to confirm the importance of the *industrial atmosphere* and the strength of the Marshallian model. However, radical organizational changes have been detected, geared towards an organization of economic activities in IDs of a 'post-Marshallian' kind, that is, less locally confined and less vertically disintegrated.

The same methodology and survey questionnaire employed in Italy was also utilized in Taiwan. The evidence from the Taiwanese survey, presented in Chapter 4, confirms the different evolution of Taiwan's clusters of SMEs, which have been facing particularly severe challenges in terms of competitive pressure over the last decades. The structural changes experienced in the economy have had a tremendous effect on SMEs operating in traditional labour-intensive industries. Many of them were thus compelled to shift production abroad (mainly to South-east Asia and mainland China) to remain competitive. The enterprises that decided to stay had to redirect their business towards more skill-intensive, R&D-oriented products, searching for new product niches and new market areas to survive. This pressure has resulted in both a gradual upgrading and an actual diversification of the overall industrial Taiwanese structure. Therefore, the textile and clothing sector has undergone a strong process of upgrading from a few traditional spinning and weaving products to capital and technology intensive man-made fibres and fashionable clothing. On the other hand, the rapid expansion of the information industry provided a lot of new opportunities for existing and new SMEs operating in electronic and high-tech sectors.

Within this context, Global Production Networks and international knowledge linkages, investigated in depth in Chapter 5, prove especially useful. To this aim, the comparison between the Italian IDs specialized in textiles and clothing and the Taiwanese experience of SMEs and industrial clusters in electronics looks particularly illuminating. On an *a priori* basis, it would seem self-evident that small firms from a small country would not be competitive in the computer industry. However, despite the dominance of SMEs, Taiwan today has the most broadly based computer industry in Asia outside of Japan, and it also has been less affected than other countries by the Asian financial crisis.

The co-evolution of domestic and international knowledge linkages has been a major factor of Taiwan's success: a continuous upgrading of international knowledge linkages was predicated on the development of a dense and flexible network of domestic knowledge linkages. An especially important feature is the diversity of such linkages: both the SMEs and the government have pursued many different approaches in parallel, rather than concentrating exclusively on one particular type of linkage. Common to all these different arrangements is that they are attempting to complement the speed and flexibility of smaller firms with the advantages of scale and scope that normally only large firms can reap.

Thus the change and reorganization observed in Taiwan at the level of both industry and geographical cluster, differ to a large extent from those experienced in the Italian case. The comparison shows that the geographical systems of SMEs in different parts of the world have followed very different industrial and technological strategies. *Globalization has not reduced the importance of geographical agglomeration, but has changed its role.*

The globalization process, which emphasizes the overwhelming role of international linkages across a global market, is posing a substantial challenge to SME clusters to restructure, open and reach out to distant markets and knowledge sources, while at the same time exploiting the advantages of local factors and agglomeration. This book represents a first attempt to analyse these issues in great detail and with novel empirical evidence.

NOTES

1.   See Archibugi (2000) for a review of indicators on globalization processes.

2. Models of Industrial Clusters' Evolution and Changes in Technological Regimes

Paolo Guerrieri and Carlo Pietrobelli

1. INTRODUCTION

For several decades, in many countries and industries, enterprise clustering has offered a competitive alternative to the advantages achieved through a larger production scale, and through the ensuing economies of scale.[1]

The typical uniformity in the growth process of SMEs' systems, experienced during the 1970s and the 1980s in Italy's local systems, has come to an end (Carminucci and Casucci, 1997). New diversified and 'idiosyncratic' patterns of growth have been observed, and the range of options chosen expands when attempting to draw international comparisons. No common and unidirectional development pattern has proved valid any more, and different avenues have been followed to face the new competitive challenges posed by the globalization of markets and technology. It appears especially useful to remember the insightful remark of the main scholar of the industrial districts (IDs):

> particularly in the Italian experience, the industrial district has often proved to be rather a 'stage' in one of the possible different paths of industrialisation. (Becattini, 1987)[2]

The aim of this chapter is to investigate some plausible models of evolution of enterprise clusters and industrial districts and provide an explanation in light of the peculiar features of technology and technological change. This task is made even harder by the variety of visions on the notion of ID in the literature, and by the vast array of experiences of enterprise clusters and agglomerations that have been recorded world-wide. In fact some 'concrete instances of industrial districts are closer to a set of stylized facts than a model' (Humphrey, 1995, p. 152), and none of the IDs is strictly equal to another, as also demonstrated by the variety of product specializations, degree of complexity of organizational and network systems and cultural and social backgrounds. Moreover, the scope and variety of inter-firm organizations is continuously expanding in relation to the globalization of technology and the increasing internationalization of economic activities.

To this aim, we shall first briefly review the literature on the typology of IDs, and in general on the variety of visions on the phenomenon of enterprise clustering, focusing on the explanations of their dynamics and changes in internal organization provided in the literature. We shall notice how little attention has been paid to the transformation of IDs, and to models geared to explaining their shift from one mode of internal organization to another. This contrasts with the increasing evidence of cluster reorganization in response to a changing environment of globalization of economic and technological activities.

Among the crucial factors explaining the evolution of the clusters' industrial organization are the external inducements derived from market competition and changes in demand, and from technology and technological change. The latter appears especially important in the present day world. The changes in the technology paradigms and trajectories, that crucially affect the foundations of competitiveness, are increasingly shaped by the internationalization process,[3] and contribute to determine the prevailing form of company strategy, especially inter-firm attitudes and the industrial organization prevailing within an enterprise cluster. Interestingly, this dimension has often been underplayed in the studies of enterprise clusters and industrial agglomeration.

In order to explain the pattern of success, the similarities and differences, and the evolution of enterprise clusters in different parts of the world,[4] we shall explore the emergence of different possible patterns of restructuring.

Importantly, it is the whole enterprise group that achieves this transformation, not necessarily the individual enterprises. Thus, changes in the internal organization and mode of behaviour of the clusters and of the enterprises therein are expected to occur, such as, for example, a rise in industry concentration, changes in ownership with mergers and acquisitions, the emergence of leaders/followers, and the entry of new firms and new agents, such as service firms, traders or foreign investors. In other words, through such evolution, a cluster would be renewing its sources of competitiveness, which were initially based on lower input costs, some (limited) horizontal linkages with a blend of competition and collaboration and mainly external localization economies.

The following gives an outline of how this chapter is structured. In section 2 some of the main categorizations of clusters and IDs proposed in the literature are presented and discussed. It is noted that they seldom focus on the possible evolutionary paths of each model of industrial organization, and that these categorizations, and their transformation, are not usually put in relation to the prevailing technological *regime* in which enterprises operate.

In the third section these two specific features are explicitly addressed to argue that they may play an important role in the search for a dynamic theory of firms' agglomeration and industrial clusters. Section 4 presents some stylized evidence on Italy to support this hypothesis and section 5 concludes and summarizes.

2. CATEGORIZATIONS OF CLUSTERS AND INDUSTRIAL DISTRICTS AND THE DYNAMICS OF INDUSTRIAL ORGANIZATION[5]

The literature on enterprise clusters and industrial districts is sizeable, and was started by the classical contribution of Alfred Marshall (1896) on the importance of external economies for industrial districts. Then, following the increasing complexity and variety of real world inter-firm organization, several categorizations of industrial clusters and districts have been proposed, often grouping widely different realities under the same label.

In a study of the Italian evidence of how production is spatially organized, Garofoli (1991) proposed a typology of models of local development that has been rather influential on later work. This classification applies beyond the industrial sector, and is based on structural variables such as the production structure, the enterprises' size, the inter-firm relationships, the background of the entrepreneurs, the features of the local labour market, the sources of innovation, the social structure and the local institutions and economic policies. On the basis of these variables, he defines three systems for regions characterized by the presence of industrially small and medium-sized enterprises (SMEs):

1. Areas of productive specialization;
2. Local production systems;
3. System areas.

The main characteristics of these areas are the following:

1. *Areas of productive specialization*; generally, in this type of area inter-firm productive relationships are restricted, which generates a 'horizontal' production system with firms competing for the same market. They are usually recently created areas, the outcome of decisions of productive decentralization, with entrepreneurs that are external to the area sometimes setting up subsidiaries of enterprises located elsewhere to exploit some favourable local conditions, for example cheap labour. Due to the clustering of enterprises belonging to the same sector, a local

labour market grows consistently with the characteristics demanded by local firms. The development model of this area tends to be 'extensive', through a rise of employment, and propelled by outside agents such as exogenous industrialization. Examples of areas of productive specialization can be found in Urbania (SP), Santa Maria Nuova (AN) and Raiano (AQ).

2. *Local production systems* tend to be characterized by enterprises belonging to the same sector (horizontal competition) but having stronger and more frequent relationships among them, and few production linkages with firms in different sectors. The local production system is structured along entrenched historical traditions of technical and professional culture, and this allows it to keep track of the changes in production techniques with minor adjustments. These conditions of productive and socio-cultural homogeneity create vast opportunities for local economic policies. Their development model may also be 'extensive', but led by local agents (for example endogenous industrialization). Cases of local production systems have been detected, among the many in Montegranaro-Fermo-Civitanova (AP and MC), Castelgoffredo (MN), Solofra (AV), Val Vibrata (TE), Barletta (BA), Civitacastellana (VT), Erba (CO), Northern and Eastern Brianza (CO and MI), Treviso, Cuneo, Alba (CN) and Arezzo.

3. *System areas* are more sophisticated and complex forms of clusters of productive specialization, based on SMEs. In this case the local production system is rather complex, with a clear division of labour between these firms and inter-relations among those in the same sector as well as in other sectors. The capital equipment necessary for some productions may also be produced locally. Their development model may be defined as 'intensive', without a rise in employment for example, and 'endogenous', based on the exploitation of local resources (entrepreneurs, capital and labour). Examples of system areas are Biella (VC), Vigevano (PV), Prato (FI), Carpi (MO) and Sassuolo (MO).

Simplifying categorizations even further, two categories appear to emerge from these studies. On the one hand, there are areas where enterprises cluster, either due to a decision made outside or an historical tradition, and share the same environment and institutions. On the other hand, there are areas where the local production system is complex, characterized by intense horizontal and vertical transactions, and by a marked reliance on local factors. Inter-firm and inter-institution synergies are widespread and effective, transactions occur smoothly and a lack of hierarchy is generally observed.

According to Garofoli (1991), neither a necessary transition from one system to another nor a predefined sequence will be followed. However in an attempt to draw a dynamic interpretation of his models of local industrial development, they may be taken to represent different phases of the industrialization process centred on SMEs and local entrepreneurship. Thus, one may read a paradigm of a shift from experiences of recent industrialization (case '1' above), to experiences of diffused industrialization, with SME systems and agglomeration of production, initially growing in an 'extensive' fashion through an increase in employment and then in an 'intensive' fashion through a rise in the complexity of the local system (Garofoli, 1991). However these models may also coexist in the same region (location) and the transition from one model to another cannot be taken for granted.

A different and interesting approach explicitly introduces *asymmetries* among the clustered enterprises and it is centred on the concept of '*leader-firms*' and of the *constellation* surrounding them (Lorenzoni, 1990; see Figure 2.1 and Table 2.1). Such a 'leader-firm' sets up numerous inter-firm linkages and is located at the centre of them. It does not need to be a large productive firm. Such linkages may take several configurations:

- Informal constellation
- Formal constellation
- Planned constellation
- Enterprise network
- Enterprise group.

Table 2.1 describes the key elements of each category of enterprise cluster: the more one moves to the right-hand side of the table, the more the target becomes that of dynamic efficiency and competitiveness and inter-firm relationships get more complex. The role of the leader-firm also changes from simply designing the project and assembling individual contributions, to that of co-ordination, strategic planning, investment and provision of strategic services.

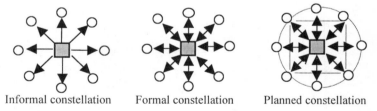

Informal constellation   Formal constellation   Planned constellation

Source: Adapted from Lorenzoni (1990).

Figure 2.1 Enterprise constellations

Table 2.1 Categories of enterprise clusters

Key elements	Informal constellation	Formal constellation	Planned constellation	Enterprise network	Enterprise Group
Target	Static efficiency through cost reduction	Static efficiency, also through quality improvements, and shorter time to deliver	Dynamic efficiency (via adaptation and innovation) and competitiveness	Dynamic efficiency and competitiveness	Competitive efficiency, that is more than simple production efficiency
Leader-firm activities	Project design, assembly, commercialization	Still leader, but other firms' role acquires importance	Not only the final assembler; also in charge of co-ordination, strategic planning, provision of key services and investments	Provision of strategic services	Provision of strategic services and finance
Role of other firms	Passive	More important: realize that their structure and behaviour affect all the constellation	More active; closer and more frequent relationships among themselves; some may play an intermediate role between leader and others	Active	Active; they do not simply execute leader's directives; diffuse entrepreneurship favours innovation
Leader-other firms relationships	Leader dominates	Closer interaction	Co-ordination	Co-ordination	Strategic interaction led by the leader-firm
Rules governing the relationships	Short-term contracts; price is main variable	Long-term trust-based relationships; price loses its central relevance	Long-term contracts, small agents' turnover; routine in the relationships facilitates agreements	Strong identification with the network: common culture and attitudes, clear difference from outside firms; easier to choose outward orientation, and reduce dependency on the local context.	Financial participation (control) of the leader in the group's firms
Factors of development and competitiveness	Presence of localization economies; better socio-economic environment would improve performance		Dynamic external economies play a central role	Strength lies in global-local relationships	Localization and urbanization economies affect the organization's performance

Source: Adapted from Lorenzoni (1990) and Ciciotti (1993).

The author does not foresee any necessary evolution across the various types of clusters. However a possible transition could occur from the first informal constellation, where inter-firm relationships are minimal, to more structured forms, characterized by forceful and efficacious co-ordination. The final stage may imply the creation of a real network or an enterprise group in the event where the leader-firm held some ownership shares in the other firms within the system. Interestingly, in all cases there is no perfect symmetry among the various agents operating in the cluster but each agent may play a distinct role and one (or more of them) leads the cluster in terms of organization, innovation, and/or finance. The extent of the leadership is more marked the more the system moves towards a 'network' or a 'group'.

Markusen (1996a) broadens the picture to include several different forms of industrial organization within the definition of an industrial district. She argues that the emergence of 'sticky places' in a 'slippery space', characterized by dramatically improved communications, and increasingly mobile production factors and enterprises, may be related to numerous variants of an industrial districts. Thus she opts for an expansive connotation of an industrial district which does not confine it to the most common usage (for example the Marshallian – 'Italian' variant – district). Therefore the definition of an ID utilized is the following:

> an ID is a sizeable and spatially delimited area of trade-oriented economic activity which has a distinctive economic specialisation, be it resource-related, manufacturing, or services. (Park and Markusen, 1994)[6]

Through an inductive analysis of the more successful metropolitan regions in the US, she develops several typologies of industrial districts that may be related to the power of larger firms, national (multinational) corporations and the state, to provide

> the glue that makes it difficult for smaller firms to leave, encouraging them to stay and expand, and attracting newcomers into the region. (Markusen, 1996a, p. 294)

The conceptualization proposed focuses on the following essential classificatory principles: firm-size, inter-firm relations and internal *vs.* external orientations. Table 2.2 summarizes the main characteristics of these four types of IDs.

The concept of the *Marshallian Industrial District*, and its *Italian variant*, was first introduced by Alfred Marshall, who noted that small firms in the same industry realize economies of scale external to the firm through co-location (Marshall, 1896). In the 1980s and 1990s several scholars resuscitated his insights to explain the superior economic performance of regions such as the Third Italy, Silicon Valley in the US, and others. They emphasized concepts such as the 'industrial atmosphere',[7] the local long-term

Table 2.2 Features of industrial district types (à la Markusen)

Features	Marshallian ID (ITA, Italian variant)	Hub-and-spoke district	Satellite industrial platform	State-anchored industrial district
Prevailing market structure	Local SMEs	One/several large firms and suppliers	Large firms external to the district	One/several government institutions providing infrastructures
Economies of scale	Low	High	High	High
Local firms' level of activity	High	Low, except for services	Low to moderate	Low or none
Intra-district trade	Highly developed	Between large enterprise and suppliers	Minimal	High between institution and suppliers
Key investments	Local decision	Local decision, but globally dispersed	External decision	In local government or external to the ID
Buyer-producer co-operation	Important (ITA)	Low	Low or none	Low
Regulation of relationships	Long-term contracts	Long-term contracts	Short-term contracts	Short-term contracts
Co-operation with firms outside the ID	Low	High	High with parent company	High with parent-company (institution)
Labour market	Internal to the district Highly flexible	Internal to the district Flexible	External to the district, internal to the large enterprise	Internal (government capital), national from other institutions
Personnel exchanges	High (ITA)	Medium	High, external origin	Medium/high (professional)
Workers' commitment	1st with ID, 2nd with enterprises	1st with large firm, 2nd with ID, 3rd with SME	1st with large firm, 2nd with ID, 3rd with SME	1st with gov. institution, 2nd with ID, 3rd with SME
Labour immigration	High	High	High for high skills, management/low for low-skilled labour	High
Labour (out) migration	Low	Medium	High for high skills, management/low for low-skilled labour	Low, unless gov. institution leaves

Features	Marshallian ID (ITA, Italian variant)	Hub-and-spoke district	Satellite industrial platform	State-anchored industrial district
Local cultural identity	Developed	Developed	Virtually absent	Developed
Sources of financing and technical assistance	Internal to the ID	Large firm	External	External (national or local government, military base, state university or research centre)
Patient capital*	Exists	Scarce out of the large firm	Non-existent	Non-existent
Local trade associations	Strong presence (ITA)	Virtually absent	Absent	Weak
Role of local government	Important (ITA)	Important	Important	Weak in regulation and industry promotion. Important in infrastructure
Long-term growth outlook	Good outlook	Depending on large firm and industry dynamics	Threatened by relocalization of activities	Depending on government institution

Note: *Presence of financial institutions willing to take long-term risks, for the confidence and information they possess.

Source: Own elaboration from Markusen (1996a) and Castellano (1999).

socio-economic relationships among local firms, involving trust and a blend of competition and collaboration, and the role of local institutions, the latter especially in the Italian version.[8]

The *hub-and-spoke* ID is the second type of district empirically detected in the US and elsewhere by several studies (Markusen, 1996b). It occurs where one or more firms/facilities act as anchors or hubs to the regional economy, with suppliers and related activities spread around them like the spokes of a wheel. A single large – often vertically integrated – firm (for example Boeing in Seattle and Toyota in Toyota City) or several large firms in one or more sectors (such as Ford, Chrysler and GM in Detroit, or the biopharmaceutical industry in New Jersey) may act as hubs, surrounded by smaller and dominated suppliers. The spokes may represent strong ties, as in the previous example, or loose ties, such as the externalities enjoyed as agglomeration economies derived from proximity.[9] The large hub firms often have substantial links to suppliers, competitors and customers outside the district. This may represent an interesting dynamic feature of this model, insofar as these 'long arms' act as 'sensors' for innovation and creativity in other locations and thereby enable the transfer of new ideas and technology to the home region. However such long arms may also inform the hub company of the potential benefits and opportunities elsewhere and drive the major firm out of the region. Co-operation among competitors within this form of ID is remarkably lacking, and inter-firm relationships occur between the hub firm and their (often long-term) suppliers, but always on the terms set by the former. As a matter of fact the hub might even be interested in deliberately playing off one supplier against another as a way of getting more favourable conditions.

In Northern Italy, this sort of agglomeration has developed in Piedmont around the automotive producer FIAT and its intermediate goods and service suppliers, and around Olivetti in Ivrea.

In principle, within this type of ID, an interesting development process may be envisaged. The spark could be represented by the agglomeration of skilled labour and business services around the hub, with the spoke firms setting up alternative and independent links and benefiting from the agglomeration economies generated by the district. In this hypothesis, the presence of a large hub firm with several activities and multiple linkages with other firms and providers would foster or *lead* the ID to venture into new sectors, diversifying away from the traditional specialization. This may be even more frequent when hubs are active in more than one industry. Therefore this category of ID may provide an interesting industrial organization explanation of the evolution of clustering and IDs through deepening product specialization and upgrading or diversifying into different products and sectors, with reorganization of production and new inter-firm relationships. It is easy to expect that SMEs by themselves, or organized within the Marshallian ID category, would find it hard to follow the latter route and reorganize their activities and linkages as required in times of radical changes in the technological paradigms.

The *satellite platform* is the third type of ID described by Markusen: it consists of a congregation of branch facilities of externally based multiplant firms. It is often induced by the policies of national/local governments to stimulate regional development. Key investment decisions are made out of the ID, and tenants of the satellite platform must be able to more or less 'stand alone', that is to be spatially independent from upstream or downstream operations as well as from the agglomeration of other competitors and suppliers in the same area. There tends to be minimal collaboration among platform firms, often engaged in different activities and industries. Differently from what happens in the hub-and-spoke version, the large, often multinational, corporation is not locally based. Constraints to the development of this type of ID derive from the lack of local sources of finance, technical expertise, business services, 'patient capital' and of the industry-specific trade associations that may provide shared resources and services.

This type of ID appears more adequate to portray the situation in the US than in Italy or other smaller industrializing countries. However its prospects of endogenous development appear remarkably conditioned by externally-made decisions.

When industrial activities are 'anchored' to a region by a public or non-profit entity, such as a military base, a defence plant, a university or a concentration of government offices, then a '*state-anchored district*' may emerge. The local business structure is dominated by the presence of such facilities, which follow a logic that is different from private-sector firms' logic. Politics may play a central role in the development of such a form of ID. Indigenous firms will play a smaller role here than in the previous forms of ID. However some new SMEs may emerge out of specialized technology transfer (for example via universities) or business services provided by (or spilling over from) the anchor institution. As for the satellite platform, this type of ID occurs less frequently in Italy than in larger countries such as the US but may represent a useful way to portray an ID emerging from a government-planned initiative. Thus the many examples of 'business parks', 'science parks' or the like, being set up in developed and developing countries through a government initiative to finance and promote a local institution such as a training centre, a quality control agency, a technology diffusion centre, a laboratory or a testing and R&D facility, may fall within this category.

In this category of ID, the growth of local SMEs, and their diversification into different industries is likely to depend on several specific features of the ID, such as the specificities of the industry prevailing, the technology in use and its transferability from the 'anchor' to local firms, and the existence of local additional competitive factors (for example local demand or distribution channels, pools of skilled labour and the presence of 'patient capital').

Figure 2.2 shows the typologies of these IDS.

Of course a real-world cluster may be an amalgam of one or more types. In order to simplify these categories even further, by singling out one key characteristic, we may explore whether a form of leadership is present. Thus IDs may differ, depending on whether all forms of leadership are absent, as in the Marshallian type, or whether a leadership is provided by a hub, a parent company located elsewhere or an anchor financed and promoted by the state. Over time, enterprise clusters may mutate from one type to another.[10] In search for a dynamic theory of enterprise clusters, could we interpret these types as different stages of a possibly continuous evolution? This would be especially interesting insofar as the latter forms of clusters may exhibit

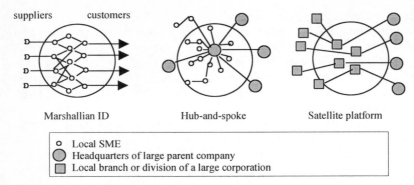

suppliers   customers

Marshallian ID   Hub-and-spoke   Satellite platform

o   Local SME
◉   Headquarters of large parent company
▣   Local branch or division of a large corporation

Source: Adapted from Markusen (1996b) and Castellano (1999).

Figure 2.2 Typology of industrial districts

propensities for networking across district lines rather than within or, in other words, greater propensities for diversification into different production lines through more complex networks and inter-firm linkages, rather than for upgrading along the present sectoral specialization.

Some possible transitions through different types of clusters are illustrated in Figure 2.3. Thus instances of a transition from a Marshallian ID to a hub-and-spoke, with the emergence of larger oligopolistic companies (1), are provided by Detroit (automotive industry) and Pittsburgh (steel industry) respectively in the first decades of the 20th century and at the end of the 19th century. These regions hosted some kind of Marshallian ID and later transformed themselves into oligopolies organized like hub-and-spoke clusters (Markusen, 1996b, p. 301). In principle, the same process might occur through the recruitment or incubation of a hub within the ID.[11]

Similarly, satellite platforms may transform into a Marshallian ID by strengthening and intensifying backward and forward linkages among SMEs that are both suppliers of intermediate goods and competitors for the same final markets (3). In the event that larger firms prevailed, or SMEs as a result of increased competition or economies of scale (and of organization) grew bigger and established leader-follower or hub-and-spoke links, then a hub-and-spoke district might prevail (4). In principle, also a hub-and-spoke might convert into a Marshallian type of district (or an infant variant of it) (2), following the failure or the loss of influence and power of the anchor firm (institution). However the latter appears a rather abstract hypothesis as it requires a true 're-democratization' of inter-firm relations and a fragmentation of the power of managing business relationships, previously in the hands of one or a few firms, among several different actors. An oligopolistic outcome looks more likely indeed.

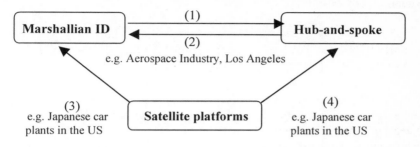

e.g. Detroit (cars), Pittsburgh (steel), Colorado Springs

Figure 2.3 Possible transitions through types of enterprise clusters

How can we summarize the very vast literature on the categorization of enterprise clusters and IDs that has developed over several decades, and that we have tried to selectively present and discuss here? At the cost of lacking precision, firms may tend to share a geographical agglomeration along three broad modalities:

1. *(Casual) geographical clustering of firms*, with occasional inter-firm linkages, no (little) experience of co-operation, non-existent or little developed local institutions;
2. *Marshallian (Italian) ID*, with smoother inter-firm transactions, much better developed practices of co-operation, more developed and effective local institutions, economies of scale at the district level made possible by substantial enterprise specialization;
3. *Enterprise network with some form of leadership* prevailing, be it a hub-and-spoke, leader-followers, or satellite platform, where the leader provides the strategic services and impetus for diversification into different products and sectors, with reorganization of production and new relationships with firms, local institutions, and factor and product markets.

It is important to note that these are not necessarily sequential stages as clusters may remain persistently different, depending on industry or country characteristics or historical circumstances and 'lock-ins'. Moreover, among the three modes of clustering, the network is the one that requires, as well as offers, the largest opportunities to reach out much further away, breaking the geographical borders without losing its identity and preserving its specificity and uniqueness. As we shall see in the following section, this feature may prove remarkably useful when technological paradigms change, especially in the new technological paradigm where we increasingly observe a co-evolution of technology, industrial structures and the internationalization of economic activities.

3. THE LINK BETWEEN CLUSTERS EVOLUTION AND TECHNOLOGICAL CHANGE

Two new major features of the social and economic systems are emerging and have characterized the last two decades. On the one hand, technology increasingly plays a central role in all economic activities and the pace of technological change is becoming more and more rapid. On the other hand, the scope of all economic and enterprise activities has become global (Pietrobelli and Samper, 1997).

These two dominant features are intrinsically inter-related and mutually reinforcing. Thus the rapid pace of technological change brought about by improvements in communication and information technologies (ICTs) is facilitating the international expansion of economic activities, whilst this process of internationalization is enhancing and further accelerating the pace of technological changes.

It has been shown that technology has become a crucial input for production, with the knowledge intensity of production growing remarkably. Consistently, since the late 1970s, intangible investments including R&D, training, software development, design and engineering, have been growing at three times the rate of tangible investments (OECD, 1992). New technologies such as ICTs, biotechnology and new materials are creating new products (United Nations, 1995) while at the same time changing the characteristics and performance of many traditional products (UNCTAD, 1995).

The second dominant feature of the prevailing techno-economic model is the widespread internationalization of all economic and technological activities. International trade and investments now account for larger proportions of national income in all countries. With the expansion of international trade and investments, technology is becoming more global as well. The nature of technology makes it more convenient for a company to extend its technological activities by sourcing technology abroad and striking R&D and technology partnerships with other companies and institutions (Pietrobelli, 1996). This knowledge needs to be sourced from different origins, as firms become less and less capable of supplying all the technological knowledge required, and all the inter-firm and inter-institution linkages acquire more importance for science and technology (S&T) and R&D. However, differences persist, there is more than only one avenue for reorganization and technological opportunities differ widely.

The literature in this area has often studied the relationships between the technology in use and the pattern of technological changes. As is well known, the patterns of innovative activities differ drastically across technological classes and countries, as far as the sources of technological advancement and the organizational structure of learning processes are concerned (Guerrieri and Tylecote, 1997).

An interesting approach to the analysis of the different patterns of innovation is centred on the notion of *technological regimes*. This concept was first introduced by Nelson and Winter (1982), and later developed by others (Malerba and Orsenigo, 1995a,b, 1996a,b). Within this framework a firm's rate of innovation is influenced by the technological (and industrial) environment facing the firm, that is by:

- *Opportunity conditions*: the firm's likelihood to innovate, given the investment in research;
- *Appropriability conditions*: the possibility of protecting innovations, and the profits thereby derived, from imitation;
- *Degree of cumulativeness*: the extent to which the number of innovations produced in previous periods raises the probability of innovating in the present period;
- *Knowledge base*: the type of knowledge upon which the firm's activities are based.

In this framework two polar models of innovative activities have been developed following Schumpeter (1934, 1942). On the one hand, the first pattern of innovative activities is characterized by conditions of medium-low opportunity, low appropriability and low cumulativeness. Typical features of this pattern are technological ease of entry in an industry, a relatively large number of innovators and a major role played by new firms in innovative activities which are continuously breaking through the current way of production, organization and distribution. This has been called the Schumpeter Mark I model. On the other hand, the second pattern of innovative activities is related to conditions of high opportunity, appropriability and cumulativeness which are more likely to lead to a low number of innovators and the dominance of a few firms that are continuously innovating through the accumulation over time of technological and innovative capabilities. They employ their accumulated stock of knowledge, thereby creating barriers to entry in an industry for new entrepreneurs and small firms. This model has been called the Schumpeter Mark II model.

Importantly, it has been shown that technological regimes are technology-specific (Malerba and Orsenigo, 1996b), that is to say that the pattern of innovations in one sector is very similar throughout every country. However one can also observe systematic differences in patterns of technological change across countries in all sectors (Guerrieri and Tylecote, 1997).

Does the technological regime within which firms operate have consequences upon enterprise clusters, and especially on their internal organization, geographical location and innovative behaviour?

It is reasonable to expect that innovators will emerge from the location where technological opportunity is available and accessible (Baptista and Swann, 1998).[12] When there are conditions of high opportunity, high appropriability and high cumulativeness, as in the Mark II model, innovators are geographically concentrated. This is also related to the firm's knowledge base, since the more technological knowledge is tacit, complex and systemic, the more that constant interaction will be needed; so one can expect a greater concentration of innovators, as this type of knowledge can only be learned through daily use, and requires informal personal contacts and exchanges (Nelson and Winter, 1982; Lundvall, 1988). This is what typically happens in a localized cluster and brings about greater industrial and geographical concentration. Conversely, geographical concentration should be less important when the industry's knowledge base is simple and well codified and conditions of low opportunity, low appropriability and low firm cumulativeness prevail. Here a high degree of geographical dispersion of innovators is likely to emerge (Schumpeter Mark I).

The prevailing techno-economic model, with the diffusion of the ICTs and the rapid internationalization of all economic and technological activities, would seem to lead toward an increasing role and relevance for Schumpeterian dynamics of the first type. Resources, capital and other inputs can be efficiently sourced in global markets. Furthermore information and technologies become generic, increasingly codifiable, and are readily available via globalization. More specifically, firms find it increasingly necessary to create knowledge through linkages with other firms and organizations.

Changes in technology and global competition have therefore diminished many of the traditional roles of geographical location. The analysis needs to move beyond the boundaries of a region or nation state, and international knowledge linkages acquire increasing importance (Ernst, Chapter 5 in this volume).

But all this is only one side of the coin. In fact location remains fundamental to competition, albeit in different ways, in the new techno-economic model dominated by ICTs (Cox, 1997; Storper and Salais, 1997). The relevant knowledge base involves tacit as well as increasingly codifiable and codified aspects. The former are related to a firm's specialized capabilities, while the latter refer to technological knowledge which is new, widely applicable and generic. So if technology can be licensed or sourced from other locations, and components and equipment can be out-sourced, other more complex dimensions of competitiveness remain geographically bounded and related to the Schumpeter Mark II model. The enduring technological and competitive advantages in a global economy are often still significantly local (Cox, 1997; Storper and Salais, 1997).

In this perspective the spread of global production networks (GPNs) may be understood as an organizational innovation which may enable a firm to gain quick access to higher quality and/or lower cost foreign capabilities that are complementary to its own competencies while maintaining an effective home base for innovative activities (Ernst, Chapter 5 in this volume).

For our present aims, it is important to emphasize that these recent patterns impose drastic reorganization demands on all enterprises. In particular, such changes are sweeping and imply comprehensive industrial restructuring, new skills and intermediate inputs. Unless the requisite new technologies and skills can be rapidly developed, competitive advantage will shift to another enterprise, group of firms or location.

From the above analysis, two working hypotheses may be singled out:

1. A shift in the technological paradigm that applies across sectors and that requires a substantial industrial reorganization is being observed world-wide. Again, firms traditionally operating within a cluster or a district would need to learn to source their technological knowledge from the most convenient locations outside it, and to reorganize their knowledge linkages from a cluster-based approach to a wider and global approach such as the GPN model.
2. The prevailing form of the 'Marshallian' ID may not be the most adequate for the new technological areas promising faster and more sustained demand in world markets. In other words the internal organization of the Italian IDs, and their strength based on local interactions within the cluster, used to be essential in explaining their past performance in traditional sectors. Yet this kind of organization may prove less capable of tackling the challenges posed by a new technological regime and an environment that demands the internationalization of production and commercialization, and most notably of knowledge creation.

4. SOME STYLIZED EVIDENCE FROM ITALY

On the basis of the evidence presented in Chapter 3 we may argue that today there is already some evidence to suggest that the organization of economic activities in IDs will be *post-Marshallian* in the 2000s, that is, less locally confined and less vertically disintegrated.

The results of our survey provide some support for the hypothesis of different paths for cluster development dynamics according to the life-cycle phase of the cluster. This might considerably affect the capacity to react to global and technological challenges and the consequent restructuring of the cluster's competitiveness. Overall, the survey seems to confirm the importance of the 'industrial atmosphere' and the strength of the Marshallian model in canonical Italian IDs. Once again it is confirmed that Marshallian IDs mainly derive their competitiveness from the use of flexible and multipurpose technologies (either 'traditional' or electronic), craft ability and product adaptability, rather than from the generation of new products.

However the evidence suggests that so far Italian IDs specialized in traditional sectors have exploited the potential offered by the global networks to strengthen ICTs only to a very small extent. In our interpretation (Chapter 3), the limited knowledge of new global technological languages as well as the lack of substantial organizational changes required by the new technologies to be effective, may progressively cut out geographical clusters and, as a result, industrial atmosphere might not be enough any more to stay ahead in the global economy.

One should point out that innovative activities in Italy seem to fall mostly within the 'widening' model of innovation (Schumpeter Mark I). Italy's technological advantages appear stronger when birth, mortality and discontinuities are high, and they would be expected to be associated with processes of 'creative accumulation' by a 'turbulent fringe' of SMEs, and by the activities of a small core of large firms (Malerba and Orsenigo, 1995b, p. 187).

A recent study on the cotton textile industry emphasizes the relationship between the organization of firms and industry and the adoption and diffusion of innovation (Antonelli and Marchionatti, 1998). In the authors' view, modernization in mature industries is shaped by the co-evolution of technological and organizational changes. In their case study of Italy's cotton textile industry they argue that the presently prevailing organization of this sector would not be adequate to cope with the widespread diffusion of new information technologies (NITs), a crucial condition for future success.

During the 1970s and 1980s the present structure of highly specialized, geographically clustered, family-owned small firms emerged to cope with the introduction of technological changes such as shuttle-less looms and open-end spinning. In those years, the Italian manufacturing industry was modernizing its production equipment at very fast rates, the fastest among OECD economies. In turn, given that innovation plays a central role in a sector like cotton textiles, productivity and international competitiveness increased following a cumulative virtuous cycle. This successful trend was reversed in the late 1980s and early 1990s, as firms' responses deepened the same industrial structure (that is technical concentration was reduced even further) and progressively slowed the adoption of technological changes. The difficulties have been related to the nature of the innovation prevailing in these years, that has taken the form of NIT.

NIT can be considered to be a technological system, which emerges when new technologies, that are individually more effective and productive than their substitutes, provide important scope for further improvements of productivity when associated with new organizational structures, new skills and new intermediate inputs. The successful introduction and adoption of these complementary technological and organizational innovations is part of a process of localised technological change. ... Only when the appropriate mix of complementary innovations is available can the full effects in terms of productivity growth be achieved. (Antonelli and Marchionatti, 1998, pp. 9-10)

Insofar as it is possible to generalize from cotton textiles to other traditional sectors, this conclusion appears especially relevant to our present aims. Every form of industrial organization may be suitable to different types of innovations: in other words, the adoption of the innovations required for industrial restructuring and modernization and the cluster diversification may be constrained by the form of organization of industry that is prevailing. It follows that the diversification of some Italian IDs now in traditional industries would require a modification of their internal organization of industry.

What are the possible avenues for such a process to occur? In principle larger firms, by internalizing stages of production and marketing, might be better equipped to adopt and make efficient use of innovation; leader-firms, or hubs in the above terminology, may be in the position of facilitating this process and bearing the prolonged delays between the adoption of NIT and its positive effects in terms of cost reduction and productivity growth.[13] On the contrary, small firms, in order to overcome such drawbacks, need to reach out to international markets to source and generate technology and should strive to set up forms of tighter co-ordination to exploit the possible complementary assets and skills, remedy the lack of economies of scale, and bear the cost of the large minimum efficient size of investment and the complexity of new technologies.[14]

In a recent series of studies attempting to monitor the evolution of the Italian IDs (Censis, 1997, 1998), the following main features have been noticed:[15]

1. an expansion of the relationships between the ID firms and international markets and agents, that is not limited to imports and exports, but is increasingly including decentralization of parts of the production, exports of licences, technology transfers and alliances with foreign firms. This

appears to occur mainly with Eastern Europe and the Mediterranean countries;

2. a less frequent entry of foreign firms (sometimes multinational corporations) into the ID through acquisitions of local firms.

In other words, the internal organization of the Italian IDs would be shifting from the traditional *circle* model (horizontally and vertically integrated organizations geared to production and innovation and located in the same, confined, area), to a *star*, that is centred on a strong and clearly defined kernel and spreading out with long rays (Censis, 1997). This would be the consequence of the growing globalization of markets and of the more competitive framework.

Additional empirical evidence is provided by two recent studies of Bursi *et al.* (1996 and 1997). They focus on the textile and clothing enterprises in Emilia Romagna, and single out three competitive strategies followed by these firms in the years 1993-97:

1. *A high reputation – high quality and market oriented* group, that includes enterprises offering a wide range of high quality products, clearly identified in the market, that sell mainly under their own brand name, with their own offices abroad or large high quality specialized retailers. Firms in this group have a smaller average size with great variance (large and small firms coexist), a high export propensity (40 per cent), and they are also very active in de-localizing production (50 per cent of this group has de-localized at least part of its activities).
2. *Traditional competitive model.* Sales of these enterprises are falling, and they produce essentially low quality, low price knitwear. They never sell only with their own brand name, sometimes with their customers', and have a high export propensity (60 per cent), mostly to Europe (90 per cent). In the home market they sell essentially to customers with low reputation and large sales size.
3. *Suppliers of large, mainly foreign, purchasing centres.* Their sales have been growing; they are the smallest firms that offer a small range of products of a low to medium quality-price ratio, and are specialized in production services to other firms. Their goods are sold under their customers' brand name, and they appear to have the highest export propensity (85 per cent); 44 per cent of them do not sell anything to the Italian market.

A central result of these studies is to highlight that there is not only one strategy of production, trade and marketing to be competitive. However only the first and the third strategies have been successful, both implying innovative efforts, though of different kinds. In fact, the first strategy has been typically chosen by enterprises capable of building their quality and reputation, mainly through their own actions. In contrast, firms in the third group have increasingly relied on the organization and innovation provided by large, often foreign, buyers, giving up part of their independence in exchange for the customers' brand names and transfer of technology. In contrast, the group of enterprises lacking an aggressive innovative strategy of structural reorganization (second group) is falling back dramatically.

Additional evidence of the increasing hierarchical relations among firms within the Italian IDs has been provided recently (IDSE-CNR, 1999), and suggests that the network of inter-firm relationships is quickly taking a more formalized and structured nature. This is especially occurring in IDs specialized in less traditional sectors, such as metalworking, where the network of relationships is assuming a more structured nature, often involving equity linkages, with potential forms of emerging leadership. In contrast, in traditional sectors such as textiles, clothing and shoes, the informal network of relations of subcontracting, interactions with local institutions and within producers' associations is not changing, but it still enables SMEs with a little sophisticated internal organization to be competitive.

Finally, the presence of new leaderships in the IDs, together with the remarkable opening of the leaders to resources and assets external to the original district, appear to positively affect the system's economic performance and competitiveness (Grassi and Pagni, 1998).[16]

5. CONCLUSIONS

The broader notion of ID proposed by Markusen (1996a) encompasses a wider range of forms of industrial organization than the Marshallian-Italian concept of ID. It appears more capable of explaining the different technological and industrial specializations prevailing in the different regions, and their evolution along lines of upgrading their productive specialization. Thus hub-and-spoke variants – with one or more hubs or 'leaders', such as large firms or non-profit institutions – seem better equipped to upgrade their specialization pattern to more technologically complex activities, and radically alter and modernize their organization.

The divide in the empirical evidence and in theoretical approaches appears to be between traditional forms of inter-firm organization and relationships versus more dynamic forms of restructuring with product diversification, progress of the technological system, and improvements of more complex relationships with firms and institutions local as well as external to the enterprise cluster.

Marshallian proper IDs, and their Italian version, are expected to be less well equipped to cope with structural technological transformation and provide a complex and articulated response. The frequent response, often very effective, has been within the 'deepening product specialization and upgrading' mould, where individual (isolated) actions of SMEs prove sufficient to resist and articulate a sort of niche response. 'Soft' strategies have been centred on product quality improvements, better marketing and distribution, quick reaction to changes in market demand and long-standing reputation.

A first and insightful explanation of these difference may be provided by the strand of literature that emphasizes the link between industrial organization and technological change and innovation. Within this interpretative framework, the hypotheses of the shift in the technological paradigm that applies to all sectors and requires a substantial industrial reorganization, have been highlighted in this chapter. It follows that firms traditionally operating within the ID mould need to learn to source their technological knowledge from the most convenient locations outside the ID, and to reorganize their knowledge linkages from a cluster-based approach to a global GPN's approach.

In this perspective the prevailing form of the 'Marshallian' ID may not be the most adequate for exploiting the new technological opportunities promising faster and more sustained demand in world markets. These hypotheses are tested with original evidence in the following chapter and cast doubts on the capability of the Italian IDs to respond to these challenges and to design and implement an appropriate strategy. Chapters 4 and 5 try to put this issue in a comparative perspective and offer detailed analyses of SMEs and clusters from Taiwan.

NOTES

1. On this evidence, see the studies in Becattini (1990), Pyke and Sengenberger (1990), and Guerrieri, Iammarino and Pietrobelli (1998), for a survey.
2. According to Becattini, Marshall properly distinguishes between different geographical levels of analysis, the industrial district showing a lower degree both in the density of territorial agglomeration and in the weight of services with respect to the urban system, and a mono-sectoral character along with a lesser degree of complexity with respect to the industrial region. The significance of different territorial units clearly depends on the aim of the investigation, although the choice of the district is probably the most appropriate to help understand the 'endogenous sources of industrial dynamism' (Becattini, 1987, p. 32).
3. See Ernst and Guerrieri (1998) for evidence on the electronics sector, and Ernst in this volume.
4. See Bagella (1996) for cases in Latin America.
5. This section benefited from Castellano (1999).

6. Her definition of an ID is clearly different from the definition proposed and utilized by the Italian (mainly Florentine) school (Becattini, Bellandi, Dei Ottati, Brusco and others) as she acknowledges several different institutional set-ups as having the essential features of a 'district'. In fact, her typology groups together several different forms of organization of production where a common geographical localization plays a central role. As a consequence of this very broad approach the 'Italian' version of an ID ends up being only one possible form of inter-firm organization, very close to the original Marshallian idea.

7. See Pietrobelli (1998) for an empirical test of the concept of 'industrial atmosphere' in a sample of Italian IDs.

8. See Guerrieri *et al.* (1998) for a survey.

9. An example may be provided by the local skilled labour pool (or cadre of business services) built up by a large firm that facilitates the start-up and growth of SMEs in the shadow of the major firm (Markusen, 1996b).

10. For instance, Silicon Valley hosts an industrial district in electronics (Saxenian, 1994), some important hubs (Lockheed, Hewlett Packard, Stanford University), and platform branches of large corporations (IBM, Oki, Hyunday, Samsung, NTK Ceramics), but it is also the fourth largest recipient of military spending in the US.

11. In principle, a state-anchored ID might also turn into a hub-and-spoke if a private company replaced the public firm/institution (e.g. Colorado Springs, Markusen, 1996, p. 308). However, we are considering the case of a state-anchored ID in greater detail here, as this form of ID is ultimately related to a state intervention.

12. Baptista and Swann (1998) study the link between firms clustering and their probability of innovating, and find evidence of a positive relationship for the electronics sector.

13. Bagella and Pietrobelli (1997) explored the hypothesis of the necessary existence of a leader-firm for the internationalization of an ID.

14. Organization changes include modifications such as: closer interaction among internal functions such as production, marketing, finance and strategic decision making; higher levels of vertical integration and product diversification; closer interaction with customers and providers of intermediate goods and services, etc.

15. These studies are based on a structured questionnaire given to a panel of selected 'privileged observers' of a selection of 40 IDs, that has been repeated every year since 1996 (Censis, 1997, 1998).

16. Examples of a dynamic form of reorganization exist in Italy, but are few and isolated, such as the networks developing around INVICTA (Belussi and Arcangeli, 1998; Camagni, 1997).

3. The Dynamics of Italian Industrial Districts: Towards a Renewal of Competitiveness?

Paolo Guerrieri and Simona Iammarino

1. INTRODUCTION

At the end of the 1970s, Becattini defined the industrial district (ID) as

> a socio-territorial entity which is characterized by the active presence of both a community of people and a population of firms in one naturally and historically bounded area. In the district, unlike in other environments, such as manufacturing towns, community and firms tend to merge. (Becattini, 1990, p. 38)

The key elements which characterize an industrial district, and which highlight its distinctiveness with respect to other forms of clusters, can be briefly summarized as follows:

1. concentration of production and innovative activities, both at the geographical and sectoral level;
2. common social and cultural backgrounds, which facilitate complementarity and co-operation between activities and actors. Hence, although the notion of competition is implied by definition in an environment of firms which produce similar goods and services in the same sector, collaboration turns out to be one of the main feature of IDs;
3. organization of linkages among business and non-business actors in formal and informal networks. Such networks encompass both static and dynamic linkages between firms – as they mark the organization of the division of labour, the input-output relationship between suppliers and clients, the exchanges of information, knowledge and know-how – as well as the connections between economic agents and local institutions.

Both general agglomeration and industry- or sector-specific agglomeration have traditionally been considered in static terms, driven by efficiency considerations such as economies of scale, transaction and transport costs, input-output linkages. However, as emphasized by Dicken and Lloyd, 'agglomeration economies clearly differ from other locational economies, such as cheap labor or materials, in that they depend on the coincident decisions of a number of firms' (Dicken and Lloyd, 1990, p. 208). More recently the approaches to the analysis of spatial agglomeration have shifted the attention from traditional, purely economic factors to the mechanisms of knowledge diffusion and accumulation established in spatial clusters of related industries; where learning dynamics and exchanges of tacit knowledge are embedded in a distinct environment of interactions among different subjects, sharing common attitudes towards particular types of learning. Dynamic agglomeration economies, which are more likely to affect growth rates rather than simply unit costs of production, have been recognized as central in order to assess the patterns of development of industrial districts and their reaction to the rapid change brought about by global competition.

Despite the common features displayed by IDs as forms of industrial organization, there are also remarkable differences between them, not only in scale but also in development dynamics and social and territorial structures. As emphasized by Pyke and Sengenberger 'it could be said that just as with large firms, no two industrial districts are exactly alike' (Pyke and Sengenberger, 1990, p. 3). Furthermore, particularly in the Italian experience, the industrial district has often proved to be rather a 'stage' in one of the possible different paths of industrialization, providing support to the choice of the district to help understand the 'endogenous sources of industrial dynamism' (Becattini, 1987, p. 32).

Most of the literature agrees that technological expertise and competence are fundamental differentiating factors for the sustainable competitiveness of industrial districts. Processes of collective and interactive learning reinforce the characteristics of the district, which could result however in either enhanced competitiveness – as far as upgrading of specialization patterns and/or diversification in faster growing fields of activity occur – or in a locking-in process, causing stagnation and decline of previously flourishing districts.

Yet it seems essential to understand whether the balance between collaboration and competition within the district, along with the structure and the degree of openness of local networks, can generate reactions to major external changes (such as new technological trajectories brought about by radical innovations, globalization of production and innovation, and so on), thus securing successful transformations.

In this regard, the aim of this chapter is to provide an attempt to investigate whether a renewal of competitiveness has occurred in Italian IDs and what sort of path has been followed by SMEs located in the district to cope with the increasing global competition. In fact, in the last two decades, the internationalization of markets, the multinationalization of production and the radical technological innovation have interacted in urging the restructuring of Italian IDs, affecting them in different ways according to the phase of the district in the life-cycle. The reaction to the global competitive challenge during the 1980s and the 1990s seems to have confirmed the relative strength of the Italian ID model (that is, based upon the typical Marshallian model),[1] in spite of the differences that may be found among IDs even specialized in the same industrial sector. However, as a consequence of the rise of new critical factors for competitive success, and of the rapid shift towards information and communication technologies (ICTs), some new tendencies are emerging in the organization of production and in the structure of inter-firm linkages which are likely to alter dramatically the traditional ID configuration.

This chapter is divided into six sections. The next section outlines the main changes undergone by the conventional model of ID in Italy during the last two decades, as a consequence of internationalization and globalization processes. Since the focus here is upon the textiles and clothing industry, well represented by Italian IDs, section 3 illustrates the principal patterns and phases of evolution of IDs specialized in the sector under consideration. Section 4 reports sources and constraints linked to the identification of IDs as well as the methodology used for our empirical investigation, while section 5 provides the results of a direct survey carried out in three Italian IDs specialized in textiles and clothing. Finally, section 6 presents some concluding remarks and highlights further questions for future research.

2. INDUSTRIAL DISTRICTS AND THE CHANGING CONDITIONS FOR COMPETITIVENESS

The ongoing processes of internationalization and globalization of production and technology have brought about relevant changes in the location and organization of economic activities, altering some of the specific features traditionally characterizing Italian industrial districts. The observation of such changes in the location choices and in the growth strategies of firms has suggested a revision of the approach to IDs, increasingly focused on the relationships between the firm and the territorial system rather than on the system itself (Gobbo, 1989). In fact global competition has rendered less momentous the traditional externalities at work in the district, attaching more relevance to the strategic variables of knowledge and technology and actually shifting the type of evolution of the district from an 'extensive' pattern of growth (that is, based on increasing volumes of production, exports, employment and productions units) towards an 'intensive' type of development (that is, based on strategic factors, sometimes leading to a decline in both employment and number of firms) (Carminucci and Casucci, 1997).

The life-cycle theory of industrial clusters indicates three different stages of growth: birth, expansion and maturity. Particularly in the Italian case, which somehow appears as structured and mature as in few other cases, it seems important to give account of the differences between 'older' districts, whose industrial roots often date back to the 19th century (and even before), and 'younger' districts, which in some cases have shown a very dynamic export performance in spite of relatively small shares of national exports (Viesti, 1996, 1997).

As commonly argued in the literature, the benefits of sectoral specialization depend upon the phase of the ID in the life-cycle: if it is in the birth phase, then specialization in one sector is advantageous; if it is in a phase of expansion or, even more, of maturity, then specialization might become less desirable. The latter stage in particular is usually characterized by a progressive enfeeblement of competitive advantages built on specific forms of labour division and organization in the district (Utili, 1989). On the other hand, sectoral specialization and labour division in the ID are strongly influenced by transformations in the general competitive environment and by the development of innovative processes, particularly when these take place at a faster pace than ever before.

As it turns out from the theoretical literature, technological shifts play a crucial role in determining the decline/resurgence of competitiveness in geographical clusters of economic activities. Especially in the maturity phase, the loss of competitiveness might be attributed not only to congestion effects, but also to the lack of new entrants in newer sectors, utilizing newer technologies. The restructuring of old districts, more than the traditional price mechanism (in the declining cluster costs fall, but so too do benefits), might be due to the convergence between old and new technologies (Swann, 1997). If the latter converge, or integrate with each other, spillovers generated even in an old specialized district may attract entry into different sectors, thus causing a shift in the specialization of the district – that is a process of diversification – and the renewal of competitiveness. Also Brezis and Krugman (1993) stress the importance of technological shifts. They identify, as the key external economies supporting the development of clusters, the learning effects associated with the geographical concentration of industries. As long as the technology of an industry undergoes what the two authors label 'normal' progress – that is something that is built on previous experience and ideas – the industrial centre will tend to preserve its leadership. However when a major technological change intervenes, creating discontinuity with the past trajectories, centripetal forces might be weakened, thus causing the decline of the old pattern of competitiveness and the rise of new centres.

Moreover, not only globalization processes but also more specific events may generate a pressure for change to adapt to the new competitive climate. Such has been the effect of the Single European Market and the pursuit of economic and monetary union in the EU, which have spurred the reorganization/rationalization of the spatial distribution of economic activities, reshaping the relationships between firms and territory within the whole Union.

As it turns out from a number of surveys recently carried out in Italy (Censis, 1997; Istat, 1997; Istituto Tagliacarne and Unioncamere, 1997), the bulk of firms located in industrial districts undertook, during the 1980s and the 1990s, a significant process of restructuring, showing a greater capacity of reaction and adaptation to the new market conditions than the average of small and medium enterprises (SMEs) not belonging to specific geographical clusters. In broad terms, three main challenges may be outlined, to which IDs have replied (or have to reply) through time:

1. internationalization of markets and tougher technological competition, which have taken off particularly from the 1980s onwards;
2. globalization of production and innovation, which has consolidated its peculiar feature of 'interrelatedness' especially since the early 1990s;
3. the breaking through of the ICT paradigm, whose effects are likely to be fully displayed over the next decade.

Particularly during the 1980s, the Italian IDs show on average a stronger propensity to upgrade their production specialization. The majority of districts have indeed reacted to demand and market changes with the expansion of product ranges, shifting specialization into subgroups of products within the same sector, and/or improving product quality and value added per unit through product differentiation and the introduction of minor or incremental innovations. Although the rigidity shown towards actual shifts of specialization in different and newer sectors with higher technological content has been indicated as one of the main constraints affecting the strategic culture of the district, it should be noted that processes of diversification have indeed occurred, particularly towards sectors which are complementary and related to the original specialization of the district.

Yet the growing interdependence between SMEs operating in traditional sectors and machinery and mechanical equipment producers within the ID has played a fundamental role, especially during the 1980s (Barca and

Magnani, 1989), due to various crucial factors:

1. Italy is a world leader in the mechanical sector, which has become since the postwar period a point of strength in the country's competitiveness pattern, reinforcing over time and integrating with different production contexts within the national territory;
2. part of the mechanical industry can be strictly defined as 'induced by the district'. In fact, the linkages between machinery and equipment and lighter manufacturing have developed within geographically concentrated systems of SMEs, thus are strongly influenced by the dominant productive culture of the ID and 'derived' from competencies and knowledge in traditional productions (Conti and Menghinello, 2000);
3. technological progress embodied in machinery and equipment represents a significant source of technological innovation in Italian manufacturing in general, and the most important source for many SMEs operating in supplier-dominated sectors which do not show an autonomous innovative capacity (Santarelli, Sterlacchini and Quaglia, 1991).

Hence, during this first phase of evolution the removal of trade barriers and the overall liberalization of markets has pushed IDs to react along an 'in line' path, allowing an internal (intra-ID) restructuring of competitiveness without changing the typical features upon which IDs had based their success. This finds some support in the fact that the outstanding growth of exports registered in the early 1990s by the overall Italian system has interested to a much greater extent firms located in IDs, exporting both to EU and extra-EU markets, than the average of SMEs operating in Italian manufacturing (Istituto Tagliacarne and Unioncamere, 1997). In accordance with the traditional literature on IDs, the better performance has been mainly attributed to (Becchetti and Rossi, 1998):

1. the transmission of information within the ID, based on formal and informal exchanges, which helps overcome information costs and provides services to enter new foreign markets;
2. the competitive climate within the ID, in principle stronger due to the narrow sectoral specialization, which fosters a greater product quality vis-à-vis non-district small firms.[2]

It may thus be argued that the maintenance of the traditional ID model during the 1980s proved to be a successful response for keeping a competitive position in the world markets.

As stated above, however, the acceleration of globalization processes, implying much wider and deeper transformations than those entailed by internationalization, has spurred what may be defined as a second stage of competitiveness restructuring, in order to become integrated in the interdependent organization of production and technological activities at worldwide level.[3] This has brought about, as already pointed out, a kind of renewal of the ID model, leading to a weakening of some of the distinct features which had traditionally characterized it. Particularly in the late 1980s and in the first half of the 1990s, some general trends may be observed in Italian IDs:

1. *re-internalization of phases of production*, particularly those influencing product quality (*vertical linkages*). This strategy, at the beginning implemented by larger firms, has increasingly interested SMEs as well, more prone to imitate than to innovate, and it has greatly affected the characteristics of the sub-contracting system in many districts;

2. *decentralization of production*: relocation occurs increasingly outside the local context, with the shift of both stages of production and sourcing of intermediate goods mainly motivated by price competition. This relocation process has also shown an international dimension but it has been confined to the externalization of low value added parts of the production activities. As a result, the role of the geographical space (*territorial linkages*) has been modified, especially where the district is in its maturity phase;

3. *hierarchization of inter-firm relationships*, mainly explained by competition on innovation. The emergence of leaders, both local and external medium-sized firms, is changing the modes of relationships inside the district (*horizontal linkages*), modifying the traditional competitive and collaborative 'atmosphere'.

Differences in the above general tendencies mainly reflect both the stage of development achieved by the ID and its sectoral specialization. Overall, the recent trends and the gradual internationalization (both active and passive) of IDs' firms have turned out to be, at least so far, a rather successful strategy, able to cope with the competitive pressure coming from newly industrialized economies (NIEs) and less developed countries. By shifting towards different and higher segments of the world demand, Italian IDs have avoided traditional price competition, betting much more on quality and design and renewing a model of spatial organization, while holding basically unaltered their traditional characters and organizational forms.

However the current stage of globalization through increasing inter-penetration of economic systems, together with the spread of new information and communication technologies, are drastically changing both the concept of proximity and the scope of competition. The capacity to foster the co-evolution of local and global linkages and networks, to develop the new interactive modes of knowledge creation and to adjust strategies and organizational forms at short notice, is a necessary prerequisite for competitive survival (Ernst, Chapter 5 in this volume). *De facto*, all this implies that geographical clusters of economic activities can no longer be conceived as closed systems, and the risk of a rapid erosion of competitive advantages may turn to certainty for local systems of SMEs that fail to become open systems through unavoidable organizational changes and restructuring.

It is possible to argue that globalization and the ICT revolution are likely to have a great impact on the characteristic features of Italian IDs and, ultimately, on the role of geographical proximity. Some tendencies are arising, affecting the relationship between geography and factors such as:

1. competition, which is bound to increase due to pressures coming from both within and outside the European internal market, the pace of technological progress and the overall internationalization processes. Moreover, the above-mentioned hierarchization of inter-firm relationships affects the market structure within the district and, whilst backward linkages have proved to be rather intense in the ID reality, the observed weakness of forward, commercial and inter-organizational linkages may hamper the competitiveness of the district as a whole;
2. collaboration, which has usually been indicated as the distinctive character of the ID. The integration between local and global networks may change the ID configuration substantially, as firms seem to attribute less and less importance to informal relationships, which instead assume a greater weight among poorly performing firms and contexts (Esposito and Mauriello, 1996; Istituto Tagliacarne and Unioncamere, 1997);
3. availability of skilled work may shrink, insofar as the tendency for well-trained work is to search for more qualified jobs, often outside the district, with implications on the process of accumulation of know-how and the overall collective learning of the ID;
4. sectoral specialization, which is likely to move increasingly away from the mono-sectoral pattern of specialization of older districts towards more diversified models of production.

This does not necessarily imply a decrease of the role of spatial proximity, which anyway constitutes the distinctive 'base' of the ID, but rather the emergence of a new kind of relationship between economic activities and space, which will be increasingly shaped by technical progress and ICTs. Indeed, it has been argued that globalization makes geography matter even more than in the past (Cantwell and Iammarino, 1998). The significance of the 'local dimension' of an innovative system has emerged as the logical consequence of the interactive model of technological change (Kline and Rosenberg, 1986), which puts the emphasis on the relations with information sources external to the firm. Such relations – between firms and science infrastructure, between producers and users at inter-firm level and between firms and institutional environments and organizations – are strongly influenced by spatial proximity mechanisms that favour processes of polarization and cumulativeness (Lundvall, 1988; von Hippel, 1988). However factors such as those outlined above stress the need for a better understanding of the ID model and its possible evolution in the new global context.

3. ITALIAN IDs IN THE TEXTILE AND CLOTHING INDUSTRY: RECENT EVOLUTION AND CURRENT TRENDS

The choice of textiles and clothing as a representative industry in the overall Italian pattern of specialization is based upon its essential significance in the competitive position of the country since the Second World War. It is beyond the aim of this chapter to describe the development of the industry and its intrinsic association with the success of the *made in Italy* in traditional and mature sectors over time. Up to now both its contribution to the country's GDP and exports and its highly localized character justify the reference to the industry in the study of IDs dynamics.[4] In fact, the sector under examination is the most representative of local systems in Italy.[5] This obviously stems from the absolute size of the sector in the country's export pattern, but it is also due to specific characteristics. As reported below, by taking into account textiles, knitwear and clothing separately, a rather different degree of geographical concentration emerges (see Table 3.1), with the highest concentration in textiles, where only seven systems (ten provinces) are found. The export capacity in knitwear and, even to a greater extent, in clothing is more geographically dispersed, as 15 systems and 23 provinces contributed to 83 per cent of Italian exports in 1995 (Conti and Menghinello, 1996; Viesti, 1996).

The textile and clothing industry shows also a remarkable degree of internationalization: the average export propensity was 24.4 per cent in the period 1987-89 and it increased constantly to reach over 33 per cent in the years 1995-97 (above that of total manufacturing, 31 per cent).[6] As far as foreign direct investments are concerned, in 1996 the textile and clothing industry accounted for 13 per cent of both inward and outward flows: it was

Table 3.1 Contribution of local systems to national exports in the textiles and clothing industry – Italy, 1986 and 1995

Sector	No. of local Systems	No. of provinces	1986 shares (% of nat. exports)	1995 shares (% of nat. exports)
Textiles	7	10	77.0	84.5
Knitwear	10	15	73.5	79.8
Clothing	15	23	68.1	83.1

Source: Adapted from Viesti (1997, Tab.3).

the fourth receiving manufacturing sector (behind radio, TV and communication equipment, mechanical products and miscellaneous manufacturing), and it was ranked as the third investing sector (following mechanical products and miscellaneous manufacturing), strengthening the tendency towards de-localization of stages of production particularly towards Central and Eastern European countries and China (Eurostat, 1998).

It is worth remembering that the location and structure of sectors such as silk and wool, which in the Italian case are often at the origin of the industry here investigated, were forged by classical location and agglomeration forces of the Weber's type, operating since the industrial revolution. Therefore the historical evolution of textiles and clothing concerns a specific type of ID,[7] which differs substantially from the growth patterns of 'younger' districts specialized in the same broad industry (Nuti, 1992).

Several studies (Moda Industria, 1997a,b, 1998) have highlighted the different steps undertaken by textiles and clothing IDs in renewing their competitiveness over time. In line with the evolution of the general model of ID, reported in section 2, the first stage of restructuring, which started during the 1980s, showed the following main features:

1. 'personalization' of products, that is, increasing and faster product differentiation, both horizontal and vertical, in order to meet a highly diversified and rapidly mutable structure of consumers' preferences. The shift from horizontal to vertical product differentiation has brought about substantial transformations in the competitive environment within the textiles and clothing districts, basically changing the 'price' competition into 'quality' competition and ensuring the successful performance in international markets;
2. greater flexibility – implied by globalization processes – in *the management of differences*, both internal and external to the firm. This is consistent with what has been observed for general agglomerations of SMEs, shifting the attention towards formal and informal networks, for

example the integration between internal and external forces, between the firm and the territorial system;

3. acquisition of technological advantages, stemming from the diffusion of micro-electronics and, more specifically, from industrial machinery and equipment which have allowed a higher degree of automation of production processes (Santarelli, Sterlacchini and Quaglia, 1991). It has been demonstrated that, particularly during periods of technological 'turbulence', investment in mechanical machinery contributed substantially, if not exclusively, to the rate of innovation of Italian SMEs in traditional low- and medium-tech sectors.[8]

In fact, the restructuring of competitiveness by means of diversification processes in textiles and clothing IDs seems to have mainly occurred through the specialization, within the ID, in complementary sectors, such as machinery and equipment for textiles and clothing. The technological level of the latter products thus strikingly increased during the 1980s mainly because of the exploitation of embodied technology – in particular, computer controlled technologies – so that the industry has been defined as an increasingly *knowledge intensive* industry. New machines and innovative plants have been associated with: product/process innovations; firm-specific innovations deriving from the interaction between machinery users and suppliers; introduction of Computer Assisted Manufacturing (CAM), Computer Assisted Design (CAD) and CAD/CAM; increase in both computerization and automation levels; higher quality and differentiation of products and internalization of phases of production (Santarelli, Sterlacchini and Quaglia, 1991).

ID firms purchase their machinery (or part thereof) from local dealers or directly from producers, either local or national, and only in a few cases do they turn to imports. The relationship between textiles and clothing firms and machinery producers is very tight, based upon continuous collaboration to develop new fashion trends. Clearly, the role of spatial proximity and the existence of long-term connections are crucial factors, allowing regular interaction, facilitating comprehension and providing an important source of knowledge for the ID as a socio-economic context. It is worth noting however that the relatively high rate of entry and exit in the textile and clothing industry has also generated a flourishing second-hand machinery market – in IDs there are often several traders who buy machinery and equipment from firms closing down – which may have negatively affected the adoption of new and more technologically advanced production processes (Santarelli, Sterlacchini and Quaglia, 1991; Frova, 1996).

During the 1990s the process of relocation in textiles and clothing involved mainly medium-sized firms located in 'older' IDs and operating in ennobling and spinning phases, which have, at the same time, re-internalized technology-intensive stages of the production process. The most quoted example is Prato, which has, however, recorded a more significant increase in external sourcing of raw intermediate goods (then refined within the area) than in decentralization of production or production phases. Indeed, the incidence of raw materials on final production has constantly decreased for the industry as a whole since the second half of the 1970s, also in comparison with other industries. In general terms IDs have undergone changes in the production structure principally by losing many upstream phases through relocation outside, very often abroad, and increasing their specialization in downstream stages of production, characterized by higher value added (Carminucci and Casucci, 1997).

With regards to the hierarchization of inter-firm relationships, the rise of groups of firms referring to a leader (occasionally a multinational) is on average oriented towards the establishment of partnerships, without affecting the ownership of the firm. This is evident particularly in mature IDs – such as Prato, Como, Carpi – leading to more formal and long-term subcontracting linkages, once essentially founded on occasional and short-term contractual relationships. The less 'democratic' structure of production organization is in fact more suitable for facing the intense international competition, insofar as hierarchization helps boost the merging between local and global networks, which is a crucial mechanism to participate in the worldwide process of creation and diffusion of technological innovation. However the hierarchization of inter-firm relationships is much less pronounced in 'younger' districts specialized in textiles and clothing – such as those in the areas of Teramo, Pesaro and Isernia – which, indeed, show a diffused 'economic democracy', with many actors operating on an equal standing, and where firms implement a strategy of repositioning in small market segments (niches) with a higher degree of protection. Although in recent years some newer IDs have registered an outstanding export performance, the almost absolute lack of internationalization and organizational change may seriously jeopardize their survival in the global market, in which the difficulty of competing on labour cost terms – particularly vis-à-vis the comparative advantage of low-cost less developed countries (LDCs) and economies in transition – is becoming almost prohibitive. As emphasized by Dicken 'global shifts in the textiles and clothing industries exemplify many of the intractable issues facing today's world economy, particularly the trade tensions between developed and developing economies' (Dicken, 1998, p. 283).

Furthermore, notwithstanding the central role played by embodied technological progress in the last two decades, it is clear that ICTs represent the breakthrough of a new technological paradigm and the main 'communication challenge' which has to be faced by all economic and social actors. The increasing networking in business relationships and the spread of ICTs will radically change the traditional means of collaboration operating inside the district through formal and informal exchanges, possibly causing the lagging behind of those IDs which fail to be integrated in global production and information networks.

4. THE IDENTIFICATION OF IDs FOR EMPIRICAL INVESTIGATION: METHODOLOGICAL ISSUES

The geographical identification of industrial districts in the Italian case is not straightforward, as the levels of the province and the commune usually overlap and none of them turns out to be the most appropriate to describe a specific local system. In fact, as Becattini indicates, the Italian industrial district is often an intermediate area between the commune and the province, normally consisting of more than one commune and often spreading over two and even more provinces.

Therefore the identification of industrial districts to be selected in order to carry out the direct survey was derived from various sources, such as recent literature on IDs, surveys and empirical analyses. Essential pieces of information were gathered from studies on the contribution to Italian exports – at the level of province and groups of provinces – carried out by some scholars on behalf of ICE (Conti, 1994; Conti and Menghinello, 1995, 1996; Viesti 1996, 1997), and from the 'Report on Enterprises and Local Economies' (Istituto Tagliacarne and Unioncamere, 1997). Notwithstanding the limits, the choice of the province as unit of analysis seems to represent a good approximation of geographical agglomerations such as IDs. The analysis of data published by Istat, not reported in the present chapter,[9] allowed us to elicit both the structural characters of production and export specialization of local systems and, more importantly, their dynamics in terms of performance during the 1980s and the 1990s. This is particularly important insofar as the aim here is to shed some light, with regard to the textiles and clothing industry, on the possible geographical differences in the restructuring of competitiveness.[10] The results in terms of export performance, confronted with other studies on local innovation, competitiveness and openness, have provided a list of industrial districts to be considered in order to choose the firms to be surveyed.

The choice of the three case-studies was driven by criteria such as:

- the identification of the 'dominant' industry in the specialization pattern of the industrial district, for example textiles and/or clothing as the

dominant industry;
- variety of historical backgrounds (search for 'older' and 'younger' IDs);
- variety of characteristics and performance;
- features of the overall export performances (including related sectors such as machinery and equipment for textiles and clothing);
- sub-sectoral composition of exports (based on the sub-sectoral breakdown into 42 groups of products in 'textiles and clothing').

In spite of the *caveat* implied by this exercise, Prato and Carpi were chosen as representative of 'older' districts, whilst Teramo was selected as an example of a 'younger' ID.

In the next section the results of the interviews for selected firms located in the three IDs are reported, in an attempt to identify a few examples which could support the hypothesis of different paths towards the restructuring of competitiveness and the adaptation to changes brought about by globalization and technological progress. The picture which emerges provides an initial and provisional basis to envisage whether the conditions for future competitiveness are met and which are the main risks for the Italian ID model. Notwithstanding the limits of the present analysis, our main concern has been to avoid ending up by describing as 'local' what is rather 'sectoral' and, therefore, more general and not so much influenced by geographical and social proximity.

5. THE RESULTS OF INTERVIEWS OF SMEs IN THE IDs OF PRATO, TERAMO AND CARPI

The data presented in this section are based upon the evidence from the interviews – carried out by means of a structured questionnaire sent to 22 firms located in Prato, 15 firms in Teramo (most of them concentrated in the ID of S. Egidio Val Vibrata) and 11 in the ID of Carpi, for an overall number of 48 interviews. The interviews were carried out in the summer and autumn of 1998 on the basis of EU-harmonized questionnaires administered to a random sample of textiles and clothing SMEs, as the maximum number of employees in the selected firms were 180.

The average age of the surveyed firms turns out to be higher in Prato – with half of the interviewed firms established before 1970 – and in Carpi, whilst in Teramo the year of establishment was on average in the late 1970s. As far as the main product sold by the firms is concerned in the case of Prato the bulk of firms (19 out of 22) are clearly specialized in the textile sector, mainly in wool and cotton textiles – in which the district showed, in 1996, the highest values (between 0.8 and 1) of the index of revealed comparative advantage (RCA) relative to Italy as a whole – with a few of them producing textiles of artificial and synthetic fibres.[11] The surveyed firms located in Carpi sell products in both the textiles and clothing sectors, with four out of 11 firms producing knitwear of both natural textile fibres and synthetic fibres (which belong to textiles) with the remaining firms specializing in garments. Teramo's SMEs operate entirely in clothing.[12] The narrow specialization profile of the latter district, which guided our choice in the selection of firms issued with the questionnaire, may have been rather advantageous given the relative early phase in the life-cycle of the cluster, at least in comparison with the other two cases.[13]

As far as the structural features of the sample of firms are concerned, the value of plants and equipment by ID varies from 100 million up to 10 billion Italian lira for Prato and Teramo, whilst the average value is lower in the case of Carpi.[14]

In spite of the greater number of interviews carried out in Prato, the total number of employees for all 22 firms is relatively lower, due to the large presence in the Prato sample of very small firms (below 21 employees).[15] This holds also in the case of Carpi, in which seven firms out of 11 are below the threshold of 21 employees and where only one employs more than 40 workers. The average firm size of the sample in Teramo is, instead, the highest, with seven interviewed firms having between 21 and 40 employees and four falling in the class of over 40. Very small variations, in terms of number of employees, were registered over the period considered by the survey (1995-97) in all the firms in the three districts.

The aggregate value of total sales for all firms shows a comparatively better performance of the surveyed SMEs located in Prato, for which an increasing trend was observed over the three years, relative to an almost stable pattern in Teramo and a rather strong increase of Carpi's sales between 1995 and 1996, followed however by a decline in 1997. The percentage of total sales directed to foreign markets confirms a much higher trade orientation in the case of Prato – where 54 per cent (average 1995-97) of interviewed firms' sales were exported – than in Teramo – with the lowest share of exports on total sales (17 per cent) – while for Carpi's firms about one third of their total sales was exported. The respondents were asked to indicate, in percentage terms, the geographical destination of their exports. Figure 3.1 shows that more than 62 per cent of the overall samples' exports (48 firms) in 1997 went to European markets, of which 54.2 per cent were to the EU and 8.1 per cent to non-EU countries (mainly Central and Eastern European countries). Asia gets almost 9 per cent, whilst the rest of the world accounts for 7.5 per cent of exports of all interviewed firms. North America is relatively less important as a market of destination, absorbing less than 5 per cent of total exports.[16]

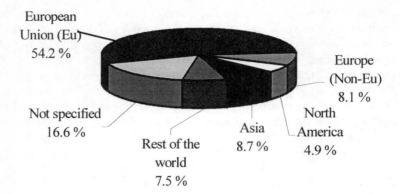

Figure 3.1   Export orientation, 1997 (average % of exports by market of destination, all sample firms)

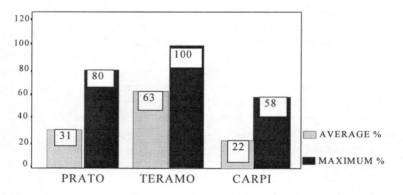

Figure 3.2 Output sold to top 3 customers by industrial district, 1997 (average and maximum % sold to top 3, all sample firms)

Furthermore, Figure 3.2 reports the share of output sold to the top three customers in 1997: Prato and Carpi exhibit rather low percentages, 31 per cent and 22 per cent respectively, while Teramo's firms seem to rely much more on top customers, with an average share of output sold to the main three clients equal to 63 per cent. This might be attributed to a stronger concentration of subcontracting relationships in Teramo, compared with that in the two more mature IDs.[17]

During the interviews the respondents were asked in particular to evaluate the factors related to both the introduction of innovations in their firms and the 'cluster effect' – that is the extent to which the location in the ID is perceived by the firm and the propensity to openness of each geographical group of firms.

First of all, from the section of the questionnaire regarding the background of the entrepreneur/founder, it turns out that the type of previous work experience of entrepreneurs is mainly constituted by family business (46 per cent of all firms) and other SMEs (33 per cent), usually both located in the same area in which the current activity is carried out (see Figure 3.3). This outcome was certainly expected and, given the marginal weight attributed to other types of previous experience by entrepreneurs – such as large industrial firms (10 per cent), multinationals (4 per cent) and university (2 per cent) – it suggests in itself a specific ID effect.

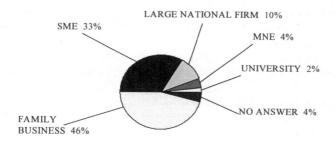

Figure 3.3 Type of previous experience of the entrepreneur (all sample firms)

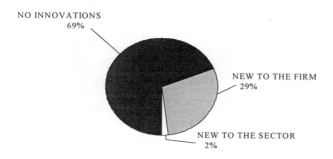

Figure 3.4 Product innovations (all sample firms)

Product innovation was classified as *new to the firm*, that is incremental innovations, or improvement via refinement and modification of existing products, or *new to the sector*, with development of new products or innovations based on industrial design. As emerges from Figure 3.4, almost 70 per cent of all firms belonging to our sample did not introduce any product innovation in the three years to which the questionnaire referred. However the rest of the sample declared to have introduced incremental innovations (29 per cent), while only one firm stated to have developed totally new products. As far as process innovation is concerned, exactly 50 per cent of all surveyed firms undertook improvements in existing production processes, mainly consisting of the use of new specialized machinery, equipment and computer-assisted technologies. Therefore, our results confirm once more the central role played by a related sector, such as machinery and equipment, for innovation in SMEs that specialize in traditional productions.[18]

Turning to external sources of technology, our respondents were asked to evaluate them by attributing a score from 1 (= unimportant) to 10 (= extremely important, crucial). Table 3.2 ranks the sources by cumulated frequency of responses which rated them with at least a 6 point score, thus indicating estimation of the source to be of a certain importance. As suggested by the table, customers and equipment suppliers were judged as crucial by our respondents: indeed, in both cases, 25 respondents attributed a score higher than 5.[19] Trade fairs are ranked as the second channel of technology and innovation diffusion, followed by other suppliers, consultants and industrial associations. Only a few surveyed firms indicated as important formal and informal horizontal partnerships, while publications, universities and public design institutions were only rarely pointed out as relevant. Moreover, licensing and government services were ruled out since they were never rated with more than a 5 point score.

Table 3.2 External sources of technology, all sample firms

Source	Frequency of response*
Customers	25
Equipment suppliers	25
Trade fairs	24
Other suppliers	16
Consultants	11
Industry associations	9
Recruitment	8
Horizontal partnerships (formal + informal)	5
Publications	4
Universities	2
Public research & design institutions	2

Note: *Ranked in order of importance.

Table 3.3 Main external source of technology by geographical origin – Prato (interviewed firms: 22)

Source	Local	Natio-nal	Interna-tional	All origins (local, national, international)	Total by type of source
Recruitment	2				2
Customers	2		1	4	7
Equipment suppliers	4	2			6
Horizontal partnerships	1				1
Trade farirs	1			1	2
None					4
Total by Geographical origin	10	2	1	5	22

Note: *Highest score attributed by the firms.

Table 3.4 Main external source * *of technology by geographical origin – Teramo (interviewed firms: 15)*

Source	Local	Natio-nal	Interna-tional	All origins (local, national, international)	Total by type of source
Recruitment	3				3
Customers	2	1			3
Equipment suppliers	3	2			5
Horizontal partnership	1				1
Consultans		1			1
Publications		1			1
None					1
Total by geographical origin	9	5	0	0	15

Note: *Highest score attributed by the firms.

Considering the main external source of technology by geographical origin of the source (that is, local, national, international and all origins) and by ID, Tables 3.3 to 3.5 report only the source which was judged as the most significant to each firm (highest score, for example 9-10). As it turns out from Table 3.3, in Prato customers were ranked as the leading channel of technological sourcing – not only local customers but also national and

Table 3.5 Main external source of technology by geographical origin –
Carpi (interviewed firms: 11)

Source	Local	National	International	All origins (local, national, international)	Total by type of source
Recruitment	1				1
Customers		1	2		3
Other suppliers		1			1
Industry associations	1				1
Universities		1			1
Trade fairs			1		1
None					3
Total by geographical origin	2	3	3	0	11

Note: *Highest score attributed by the firms.

international, as shown in the column 'all origins'; it was only in the case of
Teramo (Table 3.4) that no international linkages turned out to be important.
As many firms in our sample are either subcontractors or intermediate goods
suppliers (the latter case applies particularly to Prato, given the strong
specialization in textiles, which rarely are for final consumption), this result
would suggest the critical importance of inter-firm and user-producer
relationships. Equipment suppliers emerge as the main external source of
technology in Teramo and then ranked as second in Prato: in both cases,
however, suppliers are either local or national, which is not surprising given
the already highlighted strength of the sector in Italy and in IDs' realities.
This outcome may be interpreted also in terms of a sort of interplay between
the collective creative capacity and more formal R&D activities. As argued
by Bellandi (1996), results of R&D carried out in some complementary
sectors – such as that carried out by firms making specialized machinery for
the principal industry of the ID (in our case textiles and clothing machinery)
– are then directly tested and adopted by firms in the ID. Overall, it is
interesting to note some geographical features of our sample: in Prato, local
technological linkages are rather strong (with ten firms indicating the local
environment as the origin of the main source of technology), as well as for
Teramo (with nine firms), but while in the former case, as well as in that of
Carpi, firms also show a relatively international openness, the respondents in
Teramo do not have any major technological channel with sources outside the
country. This would support the idea of a relative closeness of Teramo with

respect to the 'older' districts (which, from our survey emerged also in terms of exports, with Teramo showing the lowest share of sales abroad on total sales).

With respect to the actual clustering/ID effects, the questionnaire had an ad hoc section inquiring first what percentage of output (both final and intermediate goods) goes to local, national and international markets, and what share of input comes from those markets. As Table 3.6 indicates, in 1997 local markets (that is the ID market) absorbed rather low shares of the output of the surveyed firms in all three IDs: in line with the evidence provided for export shares. Prato turns out to be the most open local system (60 per cent of output is sold in international markets), whilst SMEs in Carpi and particularly in Teramo, are much more nationally oriented in terms of output market. In general, the input sourcing is far less internationalized in all three case-studies: the highest percentage of input comes from within the district both for firms in Prato (39 per cent) and for those in Carpi (53 per cent), while Teramo's SMEs draw more heavily on the national market (42 per cent).

Table 3.6 Average share of output/input by geographical destination/origin, 1997 – all sample firms (in per cent)

		Prato	Teramo	Carpi
Output market	Local	16	12	12
	National	24	60	47
	International	60	30	40
	Total	100	100	100
Input market	Local	39	41	53
	National	29	42	40
	International	32	17	7
	Total	100	100	100

Finally, the establishment of tight linkages and interactions between different actors operating in the ID has always been pointed out as a central factor behind the industrial district's success. Therefore, the intensity of local interactions was investigated in the interviews, asking our respondents to rate local organizations/institutions on a 1 to 10 points scale, where 1 is equal to 'no local interaction' and 10 is equal to 'very intense, tight interaction'. Tables 3.7 to 3.9 show the responses by the average score attributed by firms in each ID. Both in Prato and Carpi the intensity of linkages with local customers and suppliers was ranked highest (with average scores indicating

Table 3.7 Intensity of local interactions – Prato (responding firms: 22)

Organizations/Institutions	Average score
Customers	7
Suppliers	7
Competitors	3
Public financial institutions	3
Private financial institutions	5
Service providers	7
Government agencies	1
Industry associations	5
Public and private training institutions	1

Note: Scores from 10 to 1: 10 = very intense interaction; 1 = no local interaction.

Table 3.8 Intensity of local interactions – Teramo (responding firms: 14)

Organizations/Institutions	Average score
Customers	5
Suppliers	5
Competitors	4
Public financial institutions	5
Private financial institutions	4
Service providers	4
Government agencies	1
Industry associations	4
Public and private training institutions	1

Note: Scores from 10 to 1: 10 = Very Intense Interaction; 1 = No Local Interaction

quite intense interactions); the same categories also got the highest positions in the ranking in Teramo, but with a much lower average score (i.e. 5), which suggests a medium intensity of linkages between the surveyed firms and their customers and suppliers. Service providers were also considered among the main counterparts by the majority of Prato's respondents, whereas in Carpi firms attached a relatively greater importance to their connections with private financial institutions. In all three cases linkages with industry associations were ranked as having a moderate intensity, whilst relationships with private and public training institutions and government agencies were recognized as irrelevant. Exchanges with competitors turned out to be rather weak, contrary to what is stated in the bulk of the literature on IDs.

Table 3.9 Intensity of local interactions – Carpi (responding firms: 10)

Organizations/Institutions	Average score
Customers	8
Suppliers	7
Competitors	2
Public financial institutions	3
Private financial institutions	6
Service providers	4
Government agencies	1
Industry associations	5
Public and private training institutions	2

Note: Scores from 10 to 1: 10 = Very Intense Interaction; 1 = No Local Interaction

Overall, our data would suggest that the intensity of local linkages, and therefore the strength of an 'ID atmosphere', is far more perceived in the two 'older' districts of Prato and Carpi than by respondent firms located in the 'younger' ID of Teramo, which attached a lower rating to local connections as a whole. As also reported in other studies, the pattern of interrelationship between firms and other local actors within the IDs of Prato and Carpi may be characterized by a well established system of networking, which not only might encourage interdependence and collective learning but also facilitate the future integration in global networks and the response to the challenge of the ICT revolution.[20] Despite the dynamic export performance of Teramo in the most recent years, its relative lack of internationalization and perception as being part of a local system[21] – hence pursuing, as such, a collective strategy of competitive assertion – might turn out to be critical in the complex path to stay ahead in global markets.

6. CONCLUDING REMARKS: GLOBAL TRENDS AND THE FUTURE OF IDs

The successful performance of Italian textiles and clothing IDs, which have managed to stay competitive without turning down the basic structure of a traditional and experimented model of economic and social organization, has to be considered as the result of a continuous adjustment to external pressures carried out by local forces. Today there is already some evidence to suggest that in the 2000s the organization of economic activities in IDs will be post-Marshallian, that is less locally confined and less vertically disintegrated.

Furthermore new technologies, and particularly the ICT paradigm, have permitted the proximity that used to be possible only within a cluster, to take place over long distances. The convergence towards new technologies and new modes of creating and diffusing innovation through networks could ensure high solidity and perspectives of competitiveness to the local system in the long term. Proximity matters and will continue to matter, provided that the industrial district becomes more and more an open and integrated system. The integration into the global economy, through international networks and markets, corporate hierarchies, global production and technological organization, is boosting the importance of functional integration vis-à-vis geographical integration, which was one of the fundamental conditions for the emergence of IDs, and which will continue to be an essential factor provided that the necessary organizational changes connected with complex technologies are introduced.

The results of our survey, reported in the present chapter, offer some support to the hypothesis of different paths for ID development dynamics according to the life-cycle phase of the ID. This might affect considerably the capacity to react to global and technological challenges and the consequent restructuring of the ID competitiveness. Overall, the survey seems to confirm, within its caveat, the importance of the 'industrial atmosphere' and the strength of the Marshallian model in canonical Italian IDs, such as Prato and Carpi. Once again it is confirmed that Marshallian IDs, in the main, derive their competitiveness from the use of flexible and multipurpose technologies (either 'traditional' or electronic), craft ability and product adaptability, rather than from the generation of new products.

Sectoral trends, however, are showing univocal signs towards radical organizational changes, with the clothing industry facing even bigger risks than textiles, due to both its more fragmented organization and the less sophisticated technological level. For instance the increasing dominance of much retail trade by large firms and multinationals and the substantial change in marketing and related activities are having repercussions on both production processes and adoption of new technologies, changing the organization and the global geography of manufacturing. The role of distributors – especially in the case of retailers – is becoming increasingly dominant and, as the global trend in the sector indicates, particularly in garments, a growing percentage of sales is being channelled through major distribution chains; the 'retailing revolution' is another crucial factor which SMEs of IDs will have to cope with.

A better knowledge of these trends is certainly required, particularly with reference to the extent to which they influence geographical clusters, together with a more precise insight on the rate of adoption of ICTs in Italian SMEs and on the factors affecting it.

Indeed, the global challenge implies not only relocation of production in search of low labour costs, but even more a variety of methods such as international subcontracting and licensing that do not necessarily involve equity participation. Competition in mass markets is still possible, provided that brand names are supported by extensive advertising. Technological innovation in production and distribution is part of the strategic equation insofar as it has an enormous influence on both production costs and the speed of response to changing demands. All firms, even the largest, have to acknowledge the crucial importance of participating in global innovation networks which entail relationships with suppliers, distributors, financial systems and customers, each of them contributing differently to the innovation of products and processes, and boosting the productivity and creativity of everyone in the network.

Yet competition will increasingly depend upon the network in which the firm operates. As pointed out by Asheim (1996), IDs with a higher potential for technological capability-building (such as has been the case of metalworking mechanical engineering in Modena) may be far more reactive in enhancing their competitiveness, possibly determining a 'crowding out' effect on those districts – such as Carpi, located in the same province – experiencing greater difficulties in readjustment.

So far, in the Italian IDs specialized in traditional sectors, the exploitation of the potential offered by global networks to strengthen communication and information has been rather weak. The limited knowledge of new global technological languages, as well as the lack of substantial organizational changes required by the new technologies to be effective, may progressively cut out geographical clusters and, as a result, 'industrial atmosphere' might not be sufficient any more to stay ahead in the global economy.

NOTES

1. For a survey of the categorizations of IDs and clusters see Guerrieri and Pietrobelli, Chapter 2 in this volume.
2. Becchetti and Rossi (1998) have shown that geographical agglomeration has a significant positive impact on export performance, increasing the export on total sales ratio by one fifth, and by almost one half when considering firms with fewer than 100 employees.
3. For a definition of the meaning and implications of globalization processes see, among others, Dicken (1994); Archibugi and Iammarino (1998); Cantwell and Iammarino (1998). See also Chapter 1 in this volume.
4. The consolidation of the strength of the textile and clothing industry has been confirmed by international markets, demonstrating the solid comparative advantage of Italian producers relative to world competitors. Value added at market price nearly doubled between 1985 (26,613 billion of lira) and 1996 (47,319 billion), although the share of textiles and clothing on the manufacturing value added slightly decreased from 13.5 per cent in 1985 to 12.5 per cent in 1996. The industrial activity indicators showed favourable results also in 1997: the growth of production quantities was 3.2 per cent with respect to the previous year (above

manufacturing as a whole, with 2.3 per cent), whilst the price dynamics was relatively moderate (1.4 per cent, though above 0.8 per cent of manufacturing). Domestic sales and exports recorded an increase of 1.8 per cent and 8.5 per cent respectively, relative to 1996 (Istat, 1998).

5. Italy has almost 200 local systems of SMEs, of which nearly half can be strictly defined as IDs, while the others are either IDs in the birth phase, or remains of declined IDs, or polarized industrial areas. However, in the sector here analysed, the majority of local systems correspond to real IDs (Becattini, 1995).

6. The export propensity is calculated as the percentage ratio between exports and production at constant prices. It is worth noting that the degree of penetration of imports (percentage ratio between imports and domestic demand at constant prices) was, instead, lower than that of total manufacturing, with values around 20-22 per cent for 1995-97 (against 28 per cent for manufacturing as a whole) (Istat and ICE, 1998).

7. It is important to bear in mind that textiles and clothing account for more than one third of Italian IDs.

8. It has been shown that in the Italian case the most relevant effects of the embodied technological progress in the sector under study occurred particularly during the 1980s (see Santarelli, Sterlacchini and Quaglia, 1991).

9. The details and the results obtained are available on request from the authors.

10. The analysis of textiles and clothing exports was carried out at a detailed level of sectoral breakdown (i.e. 27 groups of products for textiles and 15 for clothing, numbered from 99 to 140 according to the Istat classification, which is subdivided in 236 product groups) with reference to the province unit. In spite of the presence of more than one local system in the same province, by considering detailed classes of products it was possible to obtain a rather accurate picture of the contribution of the 'dominant industry' given by geographical systems to national exports.

11. The RCA index is defined as follows: $RCA_{ij} = (X_{ij}/X_{ITj})/(\Sigma_j X_{ij}/\Sigma_j X_{ITj})$, for $i = 1, 2, 3$ and $j = 1, \ldots, 42$, where X_{ij} are the exports of province i in sub-sector j and X_{ITj} are the exports of Italy in the same sub-sector. It gives a measure of the specialization of a province in one particular sub-sector relative to Italy as a whole. Since the RCA index may vary between zero and infinite, the corrected formula of the index was used to squeeze its values around zero: $RCA (corrected) = (RCA-1)/(RCA+1)$. The corrected index varies between -1 and 1, thus values greater than zero suggest a comparative advantage (specialization), whilst an RCA below zero indicates a position of comparative disadvantage (de-specialization).

12. In 1996, the share of the product group of garments in natural textile fibres (130) represented more than 35 per cent of total exports of Teramo in the relevant industry, with the RCA index equal to 0.7.

13. The birth of the original core of firms in the ID of Teramo can be dated back to the 1970s, mainly due to the push given by two leader firms, Confezioni Vulcano s.r.l and Casucci s.p.a. Their growth has boosted both the entry of subcontractors in the sector and the reinforcement of firms already present in the area (Pizzi, 1998).

14. The firms are usually mono-plant, except in the case of four firms in Prato and one in Teramo, which have two plants, and one firm in Teramo with three plants.

15. In particular, in the ID of Prato, 16 firms have less than 21 employees, three have between 21 and 40 and three have more than 40.

16. In 1997, the geographical orientation of total textiles and clothing exports for Italy as a whole was 56.5 per cent towards the EU, 8.7 per cent to the CEECs, 7.5 per cent to Asia and 8.4 per cent to North America.

17. Clearly, the results of our survey can by no means be generalized, therefore their interpretation is attempted on the basis of the literature on the three clusters here considered. However, the point in analysis is confirmed by the recent survey on Italian IDs carried out by the Bank of Italy, highlighting the scarce diversification of clients by subcontractors located in Teramo and showing percentages in line with those obtained from our interviews (Pizzi, 1998).

18. Obviously, the fact that R&D is not at all the principal source of innovation for SMEs

operating in traditional sectors is confirmed by our sample. Indeed, the expenditure on design, development and engineering amounted to only 1.4 billion Italian lira in Prato (with five firms declaring to perform some R&D); 660 million in Teramo, spent by five firms; 1.8 billion in Carpi, where only three firms have invested in formal development and design activities.

19. The number of respondents was 40, with eight missing cases in which it was stated that none of the question's items was acknowledged as an external source of technology for the firm.

20. It has been pointed out, with reference to the Italian cotton industry, that the adoption of ICTs may display its economic effects in terms of overall productivity levels 'only when associated with systematic changes in the organization based upon systemic networking among different firms and different units within the firms' (Antonelli and Marchionatti, 1998, p. 13). Furthermore, the efficiency brought about by the adoption of ICTs can be effective only with the introduction of 'parallel changes in [firms'] organization in terms of closer interaction among internal functions such as production, marketing, finance and strategic decision-making, higher levels of vertical integration and product diversification, closer interaction with customers and providers of intermediate goods and services' (Antonelli and Marchionatti, 1998, p. 13).

21. This aspect has been caught also by other direct surveys carried out in Teramo, even leading to the question of whether or not it can be really labelled an 'ID' (Pizzi, 1998).

4. The Dynamics of Taiwan's SMEs: The Case of Electronics

Wen-Jeng Kuo and Jiann-Chyuan Wang

1. INTRODUCTION

During the 1990s Taiwan achieved great success in the electronics industry, and especially in the information technology (IT) area. In 1998 the value of domestic and foreign production of the Taiwanese IT industry was over US$30 billion and ranked third in the world for the production of computers, following the US and Japan. In terms of export value, Taiwan's electronics industry has overcome textiles and clothing – traditionally the core industry of the Taiwanese specialization model – to become the leading exporting sector since 1994. This outstanding success is all the more surprising for an economy with scarce resource endowments and dominated by small and medium-sized enterprises (SMEs).

The system of division of labour between SMEs and large enterprises has been considered as a major factor behind Taiwan's production flexibility. However other factors have contributed to the success of the national electronics industry, and notably government policies. Moreover, and especially during the 1990s, networking and openness have created vast opportunities for SMEs; however insufficient R&D investment and the rapidly changing global technological environment have also posed serious threats to Taiwan's SMEs. Such opportunities and threats, and the possible available strategies to cope with them, are tackled in the present chapter.

San and Kuo (1998) present the incentive system of Taiwan during its industrial development and focus on both the textiles and clothing and the electronics sector – the two major broad fields of specialization of the small Asian economy. The development of Taiwan's industrial structure can be categorized as one simple strategy, to link up with the international subcontracting system opened up by various rounds of GATT (now WTO) trade liberalization and by the big and open US market. Over the years Taiwanese firms concentrated on production and relied on both the domestic and foreign trading firms or big US chain stores for marketing support. The original equipment manufacturing (OEM) strategy provided great opportunities for Taiwanese SMEs, due to its small capital requirement and to the low entry barriers, particularly in labour-intensive industries.

Yet together with these opportunities, Taiwan's SMEs have been facing severe challenges, registering different phases of evolution, with varying intensity over the years. At the end of the 1970s and during the 1980s Korean firms, helped by aggressive government export-promotion policies and powerful big conglomerates, attracted orders to the detriment of vulnerable Taiwanese SMEs. With their small scale and weak financial standing, Taiwanese SMEs had to work hard to stay competitive and were forced to look ceaselessly for new product niches and new market areas to survive. The challenges also came from quota restrictions and anti-dumping measures implemented by the United States and the European Union. Furthermore, by the late 1980s, several factors had a tremendous impact on SMEs operating in traditional labour-intensive industries, ranging from the severe structural changes in terms of the sharp appreciation of the new Taiwan dollar (NT$), to the serious shortage of labour and escalating wages, the loss of the generalized system of preference (GSP) status and the rising real estate prices. Many of them were compelled to invest abroad – mainly in South-east Asia and China – to maintain their competitiveness. The SMEs that decided to stay had to redirect their businesses towards more skill-intensive R&D-oriented products. There was also notable industrial dynamism, with a lot of new entrants and exits from the market: according to the 1991 census data of the Directorate General of Budget of the Executive Yuan, only 40 per cent of manufacturing firms had existed for more than ten years.

The constant pressure and the tough fight for survival have induced the continuous improvement of Taiwanese SMEs and resulted in a gradual upgrading of the overall industrial structure. However SMEs have developed differently according to the industry considered. The textile and clothing industry received little foreign direct investment (FDI), whilst the electrical and electronics industry was first propelled by Japanese joint ventures and by the investment of semiconductor multinational firms such as General Instrument, Texas Instruments and Philips, or TV producers such as RCA, Zenith and Philips. The reason underlying such a difference was that the inflow of textile and garment firms and specialized labour from Shanghai during the 1950s and 1960s had provided a base for the development of the industry in Taiwan, while the lack of experience and skills in electronics had made such an industry heavily dependent on foreign production capabilities. Both textiles and clothing and the electrical machinery sector went through an import substitution phase before engaging in export expansion, whilst the electronics industry started up from export-oriented semiconductor assembly by foreign firms.

In the rest of this chapter we first outline the decline of textiles and clothing and the simultaneous rise in electronics. Then, in sections 3 and 4 we focus on the current structural and geographical features of the electronics industry in Taiwan, whilst in section 5 some results of a questionnaire survey carried out in 1999 are presented. The role of government policy is discussed in section 6, while the current challenges facing Taiwanese SMEs are sketched in section 7. Finally, section 8 reports some concluding remarks and highlights directions for future research.

2. THE DECLINE OF THE TEXTILE AND CLOTHING INDUSTRY AND THE RISE OF ELECTRONICS

Exports of textile and clothing products started in the 1960s and became the most important export sector from the early 1970s, reaching about 27.3 per cent of total exports in 1972: textiles accounted for about 12.5 per cent, while apparel and clothing registered 14.8 per cent. The share of the latter sector continued to increase as export values grew quickly during the 1970s. However, as the electrical and electronics industry began to take off and its exports grew at impressive rates, the shares of textiles and clothing started to fall.

The structure of the traditional industry also changed over time. During the 1970s and the early 1980s the garment sector acquired the dominant role within the industry but, due to the rising labour costs, many downstream garment operations had to be transferred abroad: the share of garments reached its peak in 1984, with 58 per cent of total exports of the industry, and dipped down to only 16 per cent in 1998 (see Table 4.1). Clearly labour intensity was the main factor contributing to Taiwan's specialization in textiles and clothing and, as the latter shifted towards more capital-intensive products (for example fibres in the textile sector), the role of SMEs in the industry became progressively smaller.

In the years when textile and garment exports were flourishing, SMEs managed successfully to stay ahead of Korean competitors. One very important factor for such a success was the highly specialized and very sophisticated input support network in Taiwan. Another factor explaining why Taiwanese SMEs in the industry could cope with the competitive pressure from Korea was that, especially in garments, products have the characteristics of small volumes and large varieties, especially for higher-end fashion goods. This reduced the relevance of economies of scale and helped small firms with efficient production skills to compete and find new market niches.

However, when the US introduced strict quota restrictions in the 1970s,

The Global Challenge to Industrial Districts

Table 4.1 Exports of the textile and clothing industry, Taiwan 1981-98 (unit: US$ million)

Year	Total exports	Value	% of total exports	1. Fibre, yarn, line and fabric Value	% of total exports	2. Garments Value	% of total exports	3. Other textile products Value	% of total exports
1981	22,611.2	4,776.0	21.1	1,820.3	8.1	2,557.5	11.3	398.2	1.8
1982	22,204.3	4,603.7	20.7	1,571.7	7.1	2,619.2	11.8	412.8	1.9
1983	25,122.7	4,755.8	18.9	1,608.4	6.4	2,688.2	10.7	459.2	1.8
1984	30,456.4	5,848.1	19.2	1,933.3	6.3	3,385.6	11.1	529.2	1.7
1985	30,725.7	6,000.8	19.5	2,227.7	7.3	3,151.2	10.3	621.9	2.0
1986	39,861.5	7,296.7	18.3	2,722.1	6.8	3,787.8	9.5	786.8	2.0
1987	53,678.7	9,034.7	16.8	2,642.9	4.9	4,426.8	8.2	965.0	1.8
1988	60,667.4	9,280.7	15.3	4,078.3	6.7	4,057.5	6.7	1,144.9	1.9
1989	66,304.0	10,329.8	15.6	4,990.9	7.5	3,935.7	5.9	1,403.2	2.1
1990	67,214.4	10,284.2	15.3	5,695.5	8.5	3,190.3	4.7	1,398.4	2.1
1991	76,178.3	11,997.2	15.7	6,752.2	8.9	3,518.6	4.6	1,726.4	2.3
1992	81,470.3	11,841.9	14.5	6,939.2	8.5	3,128.5	3.8	1,774.1	2.2
1993	85,091.5	12,039.4	14.1	7,472.5	8.8	2,768.0	3.3	1,799.0	2.1
1994	93,048.8	13,999.4	15.0	9,388.7	10.1	2,538.1	2.7	2,072.9	2.2
1995	111,658.8	15,622.0	14.0	10,910.0	9.8	2,350.0	2.1	2,361.8	2.1
1996	115,942.1	15,668.0	13.5	11,015.8	9.5	2,286.1	2.0	2,366.2	2.0
1997	122,080.7	16,660.5	13.6	11,741.5	9.6	2,450.7	2.0	2,468.3	2.0
1998	110,640.0	14,550.0	13.2	10,246.8	9.3	2,338.2	2.1	1,965.0	1.8

Source: *Monthly Statistics of Exports and Imports Taiwan Area, The Republic of China.* Published by the Department of Statistics, Ministry of Finance. Feb. 1999.

those textiles and clothing firms who could not obtain a quota were compelled to look for other business areas. Some of them went into footwear, where similar production systems and low capital requirement made the restructuring process relatively easy; other firms tried to upgrade their product quality and to diversify their markets away from the US towards the more varied European market; others just shut down and were born again in completely different and more dynamic sectors such as electronic components and IT products. In the latter case, the change in production methods, organization and management was dramatic, showing that the outstanding flexibility and business aptitude of many Taiwanese small entrepreneurs went well beyond the capacity of restructuring.

The composition of clothing exports changed rapidly from low-end products to fashion clothing and knitted wears. Again, thanks to the highly specialized and efficient input suppliers, made up of both large and small firms, Taiwan maintained its competitiveness in the industry as a whole. However the severe structural changes led by the shortage of labour, forced many Taiwanese garment SMEs to move away from the country and invest in the region, with dramatic effects on the structure of the whole industry. Some firms relocated the most labour-intensive production stages in mainland China and sent back semi-finished goods to be produced in Taiwan, while others moved out completely.

Currently, garment firms which continue to produce in Taiwan are mainly specialized in high-end products with strong design content. At the same time, the textile sector shows a rather strong competitiveness in the capital-intensive production of synthetic fibres, whilst the close co-operative relationship between fibre firms, yarn and cloth producers, has allowed Taiwanese firms to withstand the aggressive competition from China and other emerging Asian countries.

The electronics industry in Taiwan has followed a totally different path of development. It was first introduced by Japanese companies in the form of joint ventures and by foreign direct investment from the US and Europe. The Japanese joint ventures targeted Taiwan's domestic market, while US foreign direct investments – initially led by General Instrument and Texas Instruments – that focused on export-oriented semiconductor assembly activities, were later followed by TV exporters like RCA and Zenith. Philips was the most important European presence in Taiwan, investing in semiconductors as well as TV, and picture tubes at a later stage.

As already pointed out, the development of Taiwan's electronics industry initially lagged behind that of textiles and clothing. In the early days, joint ventures aiming at the domestic demand relied heavily on Japanese imported components and did not provide substantial opportunities for local firms. It was only when US firms began exporting TVs that Taiwan's SMEs had the chance of massive production in various kinds of TV components. Trying to take advantage of the huge demand for such products, many good Japanese component companies invested in Taiwan as well. Such an FDI inflow generated huge spill over effects and created a lot of domestic input suppliers (most of them SMEs) in the area of wires, sockets, resistors, capacitors, transformers and many other passive components. In the early 1970s, following the footsteps of big companies such as RCA, Philips, AOC, local Taiwanese TV producers also began to engage in original equipment manufacturing (OEM) TV export activities: the quality of goods and the production capabilities of local input suppliers began to receive international recognition. Some SMEs started to export their components directly to foreign countries, whilst others found applications in various local consumer electronics products, office machinery and telephones. New product applications generated new demand for electronic parts and components, and led to an outstanding growth of Taiwanese SMEs specialized in electronics.

In the late 1970s this industry had to face the Korean threat as well. Supported by low interest loans and generous tax incentives and subsidies, big Korean *chaebols* like Samsung and Goldstar (now the LG group) took TV orders away from Taiwan, mainly through the exploitation of significant economies of scale. Facing the drastic drop of input demand, Taiwanese input suppliers had to find new products and new markets. The spread of personal computers provided Taiwan's electronics firms with a good way out. When the Apple computer was first introduced, desperate SMEs who had acquired some experience in video games rushed into pirating the products, but the Intellectual Property Right infringement could not last and the market was quickly killed. However SMEs had already accumulated some know-how about computers, thus, as the IBM compatible machines became popular, Taiwanese firms could quickly enter the market. Particularly during the 1980s IBM's open PC framework lowered barriers to entry into the computer industry, both financially and technologically. This created opportunities for Taiwanese SMEs to participate in the decentralized global production chain of the PC industry. Taiwan's computer industry initially reverse-engineered existing technologies to produce low-cost personal computers, peripherals and components. Subsequently firms developed their own design and process engineering capabilities to manufacture more complex, higher value-added products. At the same time, TV producers, who were losing their market shares to the advantage of Korean firms, rushed into the terminal and monitor business thanks to OEM orders from IBM and various other North American computer companies. At first Korean firms were putting great pressure on Taiwanese firms by catching up quickly: once they acquired sufficient experience, they usually competed on low costs. However due to the rapid technological progress both in monitors and computers the giant Korean firms, with long command chains and slow reaction to change, gradually lagged behind Taiwanese firms.

The rapid expansion of the information industry provided a lot of new opportunities for both existing and new SMEs. Existing firms, such as cable and wire producers, could upgrade themselves from TV cables to computer wires, socket producers became connector makers and resistor firms started to produce chip resistors for notebook computers. A transformer manufacturer, Delta, developed from an SME to the largest transformer producer in the world for computer and related products. Moreover there were many new SMEs entering various kinds of components and production parts: integrated circuits (ICs) designs, chip-sets, scanners, add-on cards, multimedia products and others. A massive new entrance occurred in all these fields. Thus, as said above for the traditional labour-intensive industry, there was a significant change also in the composition of exports of electrical and electronic products over time. In the 1970s electronics components, TV, and other consumer electrical and electronic appliances (which were classified under electrical machinery and apparatus) represented the largest proportion of exports of the industry as a whole. However, whilst such exports declined sharply, the share of information products on total sales abroad rose significantly from 0.7 per cent in 1981 to about 12.4 per cent in 1998, where they accounted for 25 per cent of the industry exports (see Table 4.2). The share of electronic components on total exports, after a decline in the first half of the 1980s, registered an increasing trend, thanks to the continuous rise of integrated circuits (ICs) and other computer parts and components. It is interesting to note that three out of the top five notebook computer manufacturers in Taiwan today were very small firms in the early 1990s: currently their sales have reached tens of billions of NT dollars per year.

3. RECENT TRENDS AND TAIWAN'S STANDING IN THE ELECTRONICS INDUSTRY

At the end of the 1990s structural imbalances, high volatility of OEM orders and an increasingly competitive environment, brought about severe adjustment in electronics, particularly in the computer sector. The price of computers and peripherals declined sharply, squeezing the profit margins of Taiwanese producers. In order to face the new challenges, Taiwanese firms relied increasingly on offshore production, mainly in China and South-east Asia.

In these years several factors contributed to render Taiwanese firms vulnerable – last but not least the Asian financial turmoil in 1997 – but they also represented an advantage for SMEs. Due to the sharp decline of various computer prices, producers desperately searched for lower-cost inputs and components, offering new opportunities to Taiwanese input suppliers to penetrate those active components markets formerly controlled by high-quality Japanese firms. Without such a price pressure, it would have been very difficult for Taiwanese firms with relatively poor product image to win over sizeable orders. At the same time the Japanese economy, already battered by the economic crisis since the early 1990s, was further hurt by the financial crisis. In search of capital sources and ways to re-engineer national firms burdened by massive losses, some Japanese companies became more willing to transfer technologies or release key components to Taiwanese firms (as, for example, in the case of Japanese leading liquid crystal display

Table 4.2 Exports of the machinery, electrical and electronic equipment industry, Taiwan 1981-98 (US$ million)

				Machinery, electrical and electronic equipment					
				Electronic products		Electrical machinery products		Information & communication products	
Year	Total exports	Value	% of total exports	Value	% of total exports	Value	% of total exports	Value	% of total exports
1981	22,611.2	4,981.7	22.0	2,940.3	13.0	421.6	1.9	159.8	0.7
1982	22,204.3	4,584.4	20.6	2,529.6	11.4	427.7	1.9	232.5	1.0
1983	25,122.7	5,639.9	22.4	2,828.0	11.3	515.0	2.0	616.0	2.5
1984	30,456.4	7,465.7	24.5	3,473.6	11.4	717.5	2.4	1,067.6	3.5
1985	30,725.7	7,440.9	24.2	3,038.3	9.9	797.4	2.6	1,317.6	4.3
1986	39,861.5	10,138.1	25.4	3,906.9	9.8	1,013.3	2.5	2,397.8	6.0
1987	53,678.7	15,327.2	28.6	5,731.1	10.7	1,515.5	2.8	3,781.6	7.0
1988	60,667.4	19,158.2	31.6	6,684.1	11.0	1,976.4	3.3	5,012.6	8.3
1989	66,304.0	21,826.4	32.9	8,127.8	12.3	2,190.0	3.3	4,413.5	6.7
1990	67,214.4	23,131.0	34.4	7,725.3	11.5	2,207.7	3.3	5,023.6	7.5
1991	76,178.3	26,298.9	34.5	8,183.3	10.7	2,538.6	3.3	5,588.8	7.3
1992	81,470.3	29,690.3	36.4	8,682.2	10.7	2,783.6	3.4	6,423.5	7.9
1993	85,091.5	33,474.7	39.3	10,259.2	12.1	3,217.9	3.8	6,439.5	7.6
1994	93,048.8	37,810.1	40.6	12,333.9	13.3	3,446.6	3.7	6,790.8	7.3
1995	111,658.8	48,829.1	43.7	16,250.4	14.6	3,998.6	3.6	9,906.9	8.9
1996	115,942.1	53,727.2	46.3	16,631.6	14.3	4,224.5	3.6	12,545.9	10.8
1997	122,080.7	58,990.8	48.3	18,024.1	14.8	4,767.5	3.9	14,441.6	11.8
1998	110,640.0	55,310.0	50.0	16,911.6	15.3	4,354.7	3.9	13,773.9	12.4

Source: *Monthly Statistics of Exports and Imports Taiwan Area, The Republic of China.* Published by the Department of Statistics, Ministry of Finance. Feb. 1999.

(LCD) producers, which have only recently started to license their technology).

There has been an intense debate on how Taiwanese firms, most of them SMEs, have been able to compete successfully in the international market. Abundant human capital, strong information networks among local and overseas Chinese engineers, flexible and specialized production systems and broadly based supporting industries are all commonly mentioned as distinctive characteristics of Taiwanese SMEs. Among them, the flexible production system utilizing specialized subcontractors is probably their most important strength. By using specialized subcontractors, firms have been able to minimize investment costs as well as business cycle risks, at the same time assembling necessary resources to serve large orders. Not only is vertical subcontracting commonly in place, but horizontal subcontracting is also frequently used to serve large orders within a short period of time. Although there is also a tremendous risk involved in such a kind of horizontal subcontracting (as the firm may generate its own future competitors), it has been essential for SMEs with limited resources, allowing them to avoid the huge costs and risks connected with heavy investments and volatile OEM markets.[1]

An important distinctive feature of the Taiwanese supporting network is that it never implies a stable relationship between input suppliers and users, which instead characterizes the Japanese case. In the latter model of industrial networks big conglomerates usually keep very stable relationships with their suppliers: Japanese 'centre' firms provide steady orders to their 'satellite' firms and frequently technical assistance as well. Sometimes centre firms have cross-share holding with their satellite suppliers, or supply financial resources if needed. Instead, probably due to the dominance of small sizes and to the unstable competitive environment, centre firms in Taiwan try rather to squeeze input suppliers in order to lower costs and enhance competitiveness. Particularly when there is strong competitive pressure, either from local or foreign firms, Taiwanese centre companies have to bargain hard in order to reduce costs. For this reason if their suppliers cannot meet the price target they have to switch to new suppliers. This constant pressure has propelled the improvement of SMEs, although clearly not all of them could succeed. In many cases SMEs go bankrupt: those who fail to pass the competitive test disappear, some find new opportunities in related fields, whilst many successful SMEs are bound to grow into medium-sized or large firms. This tough reality, however, has made Taiwanese input support networks very dynamic and efficient.

In order to survive, Taiwanese firms would adopt any strategy they think suitable, some even very risky. One very famous notebook computer firm, Inventech, adopted the risky strategy of staying with only one customer, Compaq. By linking up with the largest firm, it grew rapidly thanks to the large orders coming from Compaq. On the other hand, relying on a single customer means that if the relationship with Compaq turns sour, the company will be ruined: however, due to the risk involved, major efforts have been made to serve Compaq efficiently and so far Inventech has won the trust of its client, which in turn continues to provide support, even though sourcing also from other local notebook producers in the country.

Another example is that of the Taiwan Semiconductor Manufacturing Corporation (TSMC), the most profitable IC firm in Taiwan over the last few years. By deciding to concentrate on OEM-type IC production and give up its own IC design, TSMC puts itself in the position of being able to survive only if it can always be the most efficient producer in the market. However, because TSMC does not have its own products, designing firms are very disposed to ask the firm to produce ICs for them, not facing the risk of having their designs stolen. In this way, TSMC can concentrate on improving production technologies without having to worry about design development, marketing and other related activities.

The last example is a multimedia firm, Avertech, who started with only NT$5 million in the early 1990s and turned into a successful company traded over the counter within five years. Because of its small size, the company has focused on converter boxes that transfer audio-video signals into computers and vice versa: by concentrating on a single function, rather than on the whole computer or TV, this firm became a top leader in the field. In addition, not designing the whole system means that there exist good opportunities to co-operate with many TV firms or computer makers.

All the examples above show that Taiwanese firms have tried their best to formulate suitable competitive strategies. So far the most commonly adopted strategy for SMEs has been to be content with OEM production. Being small, in fact, makes it very difficult to engage in marketing as well as in production, especially in the international market: therefore, by concentrating only on production, SMEs can continue to upgrade their technologies, depending on foreign customers for all other activities. Nevertheless, as production costs in Taiwan become higher and higher, SMEs may have to change their strategies in the future, or to invest abroad in order to survive.

4. THE STRUCTURAL AND GEOGRAPHICAL FEATURES OF TAIWAN'S ELECTRONICS INDUSTRY[2]

The electronics industry includes computer hardware, electronic components, electronic products, such as audio-video equipment and communication equipment. The largest sector in 1996 was computer hardware, with a production value of more than NT$964 billion, followed by electronic components with approximately NT$787 billion.

There were 331 firms in the computer hardware sector in 1986 but their number quickly rose to 1,353 firms in 1996. However, although SMEs represented almost 91 per cent of total computer firms, large firms with more than 200 employees dominated in terms of employment share, production value and exports: as expected in the highly skilled and R&D-intensive computer sector, it seems very difficult for SMEs to be competitive.

The geographical distribution of computer firms concentrates on the long belt from Taipei City to Hsinchu City (see map). Because of the important role played by large firms in this sector, the total value of production has been taken as a measure of concentration. In 1996 Taipei City had the highest production share (45.7 per cent), followed by Taipei County (15.3 per cent), Hsinchu County (15.1 per cent) and Taoyuan County (10.7 per cent). All four locations are linking together to form a production belt, holding on the whole 87 per cent of total production and 84 per cent of employees in the sector.

Turning to electronic components, there were already 2,238 firms in 1986, doubling to 4,523 firms in 1996. Even in this case, although the share of SMEs was about 95 per cent of the total, in 1996 large firms accounted for more than 63 per cent of total employment and accumulated 76 per cent of production value in the sector. The dominant role of large firms may be attributable to the capital-intensive nature of IC production, which only large size can attain. The geographical distribution of the electronic components sector is more evenly spread than that of computer hardware. The heaviest concentration is found in Taoyuan County, with 26.2 per cent of total production, followed by Hsinchu County (18.8 per cent), Taipei County (17.7 per cent) and Kaohsiung City (11.1 per cent): the top four sites together gathered 73.9 per cent of total production. It is interesting to note that Hsinchu City registered 10.8 per cent of production, a bigger share than that of Taipei City (8.6 per cent). Leaving out Kaohsiung, where two export processing zones exist, the electronics belt from Taipei City to the Hsinchu area gathered more than 82 per cent of total production. As for exports, Taoyuan County, Kaohsiung City, Taipei County and Taipei City are the four largest bases.

Electronic products including video and audio equipment encompassed 1,059 firms in 1986, and stood at about the same level in 1996, with 1,178 firms. The share of SMEs rose from 88.3 per cent in 1986 to 96.5 per cent in 1996; similarly, the share of SME employment also increased from 24.8 per cent in 1986 to 48.0 per cent in 1996. This seems to indicate that large firms cannot compete with big Korean firms for large OEM orders or branded products in the area of TV and other audio-video equipment, whilst small firms, focusing on niche markets, can find some living space more easily. It has to be noticed that both the value of production and exports of the sector sharply declined in 1991, and the production value of 1996 could not get back to the 1986 level. Thus it might be argued that in a relatively battered industry, flexible SMEs have better chances of survival. The most important production bases for electronic products included Taipei City (31.0 per cent), Taipei County (24 per cent), Taoyuan County (15.1 per cent) and Kaohsiung City (10.8 per cent), which together account for 74.6 per cent of total exports of the sector.

Finally, with respect to the communication equipment sector, data indicate a rise in the number of firms and value of production, while employment and exports have both declined over the period considered. The reason might be that traditional exports of telephone sets can no longer compete with new (and low-cost) emerging countries' producers, and Taiwanese firms are now targeting mainly the domestic market. Interestingly, the share of SMEs rose substantially for all indicators: from 87.9 per cent in 1986 to 94.7 per cent in 1996 in terms of number of firms; from 25.4 per cent to 44.4 per cent with reference to SMEs' employment share; from 21.0 per cent to 48.1 per cent for the value of production and from 15.6 per cent to 40.3 per cent for SMEs' share of exports. The distribution of communication equipment firms is strongly concentrated in the north, with Taipei County taking up 31.5 per cent of production value, Taipei City 31.1 per cent, Hsinchu City 12.2 per cent and Taoyuan County 9.4 per cent. Those four areas largely contributed also to exports, with an overall share of 73.2 per cent.

On the whole, then, the geographical distribution of the electronics industry is definitely more concentrated in northern Taiwan. SMEs tend to prevail in all sectors in terms of their number, but only in relatively less R&D-intensive sectors do they represent a dynamic entity.

5. THE RESULTS OF THE DIRECT SURVEY

This section presents the results of the direct survey carried out in the summer and autumn of 1999 on the basis of EU-harmonized questionnaires. SMEs included in the sample were mainly those recommended by industry associations, for a total of 23 companies, interviewed with reference to the period 1996-98.

All 23 surveyed SMEs were located in northern Taiwan, reflecting the cluster effect in Hsinchu County (or Hsinchu City) and 2 in Taoyuan County. As far as the year of establishment of the company is concerned, eight companies had been active for less than ten years, eight for 10-20 years and seven were founded more than 20 years ago (see Table 4.3). This is longer than for the average of SMEs in Taiwan, which show an average existence of around ten years.

Table 4.3 Age of surveyed firms

Age	Number of firms
Below 10 years	8
Between 10 and 20 years	8
Above 20	7
Total	23

Source: Authors' questionnaire.

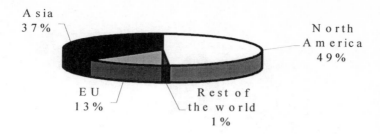

Figure 4.1 Export orientation, 1998 (% of export values by market of destination)

Turning to the sales performance of the respondent SMEs, in 1998 average sales per company were approximately NT$1.477 billion (the exchange rate during this period was roughly US$1 = NT$32). Of the 23 interviewed companies, nearly half (11) were export-oriented (that is exports accounted for more than 50 per cent of total sales): of these, there were seven companies for which exports accounted for more than 80 per cent of total sales. For the 15 firms that exported part of their output, North America was the main market of destination (49 per cent of total export value of the 15 SMEs), followed by Asia with 37 per cent, the European Union with 13 per cent and other areas with only 1 per cent (see Figure 4.1). This is consistent with the fact that the US has traditionally been Taiwan's leading export market.

The evidence also shows a relatively high concentration of customers among electronic SMEs: for ten companies the three largest customers accounted for more than 70 per cent of their total sales, for four the percentage of the top three clients was between 50 and 70 per cent, five declared a concentration of sales around 30-50 per cent and only for one firm the three main customers accounted for under 30 per cent of total sales (see Figure 4.2). One important aim for the future might be to achieve a greater client diversification.

Most small and medium-sized entrepreneurs in the field of information technology in Taiwan come from an engineering or electrical machinery background: in addition, they have usually been very successful in establishing networks with customers and suppliers all over the world and in engaging in the exchange of technology and market information in order to strengthen their own capacity to respond to market changes in both supply and demand. The academic qualifications and background of the firms' founders may have facilitated the establishment of successful networks and linkages with customers and suppliers. Indeed, 18 out of the 23 entrepreneurs interviewed held a university degree (mainly obtained in universities abroad,

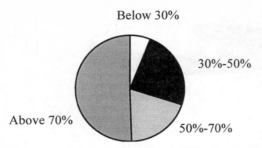

Figure 4.2 Output sold to top 3 customers, 1998 (responding firms = 20)

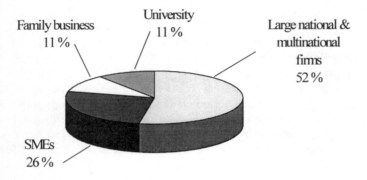

Figure 4.3 Type of previous experience of the entrepreneur (responding firms = 23)

particularly in the US), 17 of them having graduated in engineering and one in economics. The other five entrepreneurs had all taken over family businesses without formal qualifications. This seems also to support the view that small and medium enterprises in Taiwan are strongly dependent on high-quality management: a company is more likely to survive and thrive if its chairperson is highly qualified. At the same time, the short product life-span and fierce competition in the IT and electronics sector imply that a firm is more likely to perform successfully if its entrepreneur possesses relevant specialized knowledge, and especially an engineering background. With reference to the company founders' professional experience, a high percentage (12 entrepreneurs out of 23) had previously worked in large domestic or multinational companies (see Figure 4.3). This might be explained by the fact that the high level of risk involved in running an electronics company requires a reasonable level of previous experience in management and technological activities. An SME has a greater chance of success if the entrepreneur has worked in a large domestic company and, even more, in a multinational enterprise, building up sufficiently sound experience before starting his or her own business.

It should be taken into account that the life-cycle of information products is relatively short, technology is continually updated and prices tend to drop quite rapidly; moreover, as soon as a business disregards making allowance for after-sales service costs, even if the overall activity is expanding rapidly, it is still possible for it to break out with huge losses. Therefore, enterprises without storage management capabilities and a forward-looking approach are more likely to be eliminated. During the PC price war in the second half of 1991, for instance, 50 to 60 companies per month went bankrupt: the only enterprises that could survive and managed to flourish were those with good administration skills and high levels of personnel qualification (Kuo, 1998; Ernst, 2001, Chapter 5 in this volume).

The first prerequisite for a firm to be able to develop from an SME into a large enterprise is an excellent technological capability, whilst the second condition is successful market positioning. Looking at R&D and innovation, in 12 out of 19 responding firms the ratio of R&D expenditure to total sales was under 3 per cent (see Table 4.4), reflecting the fact that most of Taiwan's SMEs rely on foreign sources of R&D, and their production is undertaken mainly on an OEM basis. However, for five firms the ratio of R&D expenditure to sales exceeded 5 per cent: four of such companies were semiconductor design firms and one was a network-related company. In these latter sectors the product life-cycle of integrated circuits and drawing chips is very short and competition is fierce: as a result, SMEs specializing in these sectors need to spend relatively more on R&D.

Table 4.4 R&D expenditure as percentage of total sales (1998) (responding firms = 19)

Percentage	Number of firms
Below 1%	2
1%-3%	10
3%-5%	2
Above 5%	5

Source: Authors' questionnaire.

As far as innovation is concerned, 17 out of the 19 SMEs that answered this question were engaged in innovative activities (see Figure 4.4); 15 declared to have undertaken efforts to innovate, by introducing either product or process innovations or both (Table 4.5). Given the high level of competition among SMEs, they mainly innovate in order to reduce costs and improve products and production processes, without a great pressure to spend on research; moreover, a second substantial reason to innovate is the desire to improve the firm's organization (ten out of 15 innovative firms stated introducing organizational innovation in the period 1996-98).

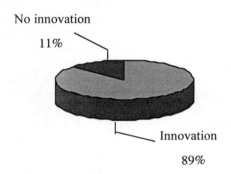

No innovation

11%

Innovation

89%

Figure 4.4 Percentage of firms engaged in innovation (1996-98)

Table 4.5   Types of innovation introduced (1996-98) (responding firms = 19)

Types of innovation	Frequency of response
Product innovation	15
Process innovation	15
Organization innovation	10
Inventory innovation	7
Administrative innovation	4

Source: Authors' questionnaire.

It is interesting to report a few examples of SMEs' development, as they came out from the direct interviews. One firm, for instance, possesses strong technology support, R&D engineers, superior product design capabilities and administrative skills. As far as its market is concerned, besides having secured OEM orders, the company has acquired a spot in the market for compatible computers with products of first-rate quality and more than reasonable prices. Another SME started as a computer dictionary company before developing into a well-known manufacturer of notebook computers. In order to accomplish this transition the firm relied on excellent product design and production capability, enabling it to secure OEM/ODM (original design manufacturing) orders. A third firm surveyed, in addition to the development of virus protection software by mastering core technology, has established strategic alliances with international giants. In order to penetrate the Japanese market, the entrepreneur of the company was personally based in Japan to promote sales and the company has effectively broken into the niche market, becoming a software producer of international reputation.

Thus the interviews carried out give some support to the common view that OEM/ODM orders have helped manufacturers to acquire technological and product design capability from foreign companies, at the same time absorbing relevant experience in product management and shipping procedures. This valuable feedback effect has greatly enhanced the learning and innovative capacity of SMEs in Taiwan (Ernst, 2001, Chapter 5 in this volume).

As far as the sources of technology are concerned, the survey SMEs seem to rely heavily on in-house R&D. Of the 19 responding firms, 18 felt that internal R&D was very important (attributing a score ≥ 5 on a scale from 1 to 10). Among local external sources of technology (see Table 4.6), the most important was horizontal partnership with other domestic firms, followed by local trade fairs, publications, customers, public research and design institutions and equipment suppliers. SMEs are generally glad to collaborate on innovation and technology with other companies, whether on a formal or informal basis. Another point worth noting, which will be explored in the next section, is that public research and design institutions established by the government (such as the Institute for Information Industry) also play an important role in transferring technology to SMEs in the private sector. Among international sources of technology, equipment suppliers and customers were almost equally ranked as the most relevant, followed by publications and licensing (see Table 4.7). As a high proportion of the surveyed firms undertake production on an OEM basis, the use of technology supplied by the customer to meet its requirements is quite significant. At the same time a high percentage of the equipment used by SMEs is purchased abroad; as expected, the technical know-how embodied into this equipment is another crucial source of technology. With regard to publications, SMEs generally lack suitable marketing channels; thus, when a firm seeks to market its own products, placing advertisements in foreign periodicals can be a significant channel. Furthermore, for some IC design SMEs, which need to use precision equipment and advanced technology, securing technology licensing is also a relevant means of obtaining technical knowledge.

The dynamic attitude towards product and process innovation by Taiwan SMEs may have resulted in a decrease in production costs. Thus, among the 23 SMEs in our sample, 15 reported falling costs and nine of them by over 10

Table 4.6   External sources of technology: local sources[*]
(responding firms = 19)

Local source	Cumulated scores
Horizontal partnerships (formal/informal)	76
Trade fairs	62
Publications	56
Customers	56
Public research & design institutions	48
Equipment suppliers	47

Note: [*]Ranked in order of importance, only items with score > 5.

Source: Authors' questionnaire.

Table 4.7   External sources of technology: international sources[*] *(responding firms = 19)*

International source	Cumulated scores
Equipment suppliers	67
Customers	66
Publications	65
Licensing	57
Other suppliers	28
Horizontal partnerships	28

Note: [*]Ranked in order of importance, only items with score > 5.

Source: Authors' questionnaire.

per cent (see Table 4.8). The six firms registering an increase in production costs were concentrated in electrolytic capacitor and plastics sectors, where the short supply of parts or raw materials tend to push costs up. Significant improvement over the most recent years (1996-98) was also evident in the percentage of goods rejected and in time-to-deliver rates. Clearly, SMEs' effort to innovate in their production processes and inventory management have had a significant impact on improving delivery times and failure rates.

As far as the interaction with other firms, organizations and institutions is concerned, the most intense interactions operate with suppliers, customers, financial institutions, competitors and service providers (see Table 4.9). Clearly, the intensity of such contacts and relationships varies greatly according to the geographical level (local, national, international): for example, with reference to interactions with financial institutions, SMEs were still reliant mainly on local or national financial institutions, having little contacts at the international level, whilst the importance of competitors emerged as significant only at the national level.

Table 4.8 Change in production costs (1996-98) (responding firms = 23)

Cost variation	Number of firms
Up over 10%	4
Up 1-10%	2
Unchanged	2
Down 1-10%	6
Down over 10%	9

Source: Authors' questionnaire.

Table 4.9 Intensity of local/national/international interactions (1996-98) (responding firms = 15)

Organization/institution	Cumulated scores		
	Local	National	International
Customers	70 (2)	80 (2)	58 (1)
Suppliers	74 (1)	92 (1)	25 (2)
Competitors	7	55 (4)	15
Financial institutions	56 (3)	59 (3)	17 (4)
Service providers	32 (4)	48	19 (3)
Government agencies	20	45	3
Industry associations	18	38	5
Training institutions	22	21	3

Notes: Score from 10 to 1, 10: very intense interaction; 1: no interaction. Numbers in parentheses represent ranking.

Source: Authors' questionnaire.

Finally, as Taiwan's SMEs are mostly export-oriented or subcontractors, they necessarily have very close links with their international customers. At the same time, as the quality of domestically produced machinery, equipment and raw materials is not as high as that of the developed countries, there is a strong reliance on imports of inputs such as machinery, components and raw materials. However, in terms of technical personnel, SMEs still prefer to obtain it locally or from other parts of the country rather than from abroad.

6. THE ROLE OF GOVERNMENT POLICIES TO SUPPORT SMES IN THE ELECTRONICS INDUSTRY

Joint R&D – 'Alliance for the Joint Development of Notebook Computers'

Given the huge potential market demand resulting from the possibility that notebook computers may gradually replace desktop computers, in 1990 the Taiwanese Electrical Materials Association invited manufacturers to found the 'Alliance for the Joint Development of Notebook Computers'. It was initially estimated that 15 firms would be involved in the joint development plan. However, notwithstanding the strong protest of the leading domestic PC manufacturers, like Acer, the government refused to set any entry requirements, except an initial entry fee of $48,000 – a sum which even a SME could well afford to pay. Following the public encouragement, 42 manufacturers joined the first round and four more participated in the second.

In fact, a number of firms in the alliance had no experience in producing PCs at all. They came from the telecommunication industry, trying to tap into a new field: their main motivation was to acquire IT competence in various areas such as inspection, testing, quality control, design, purchasing and marketing through their experience of joint development. Other small and medium manufacturers with experience in developing PCs joined the alliance hoping to reduce risks and costs, to grasp development opportunities and to take control of future technology development trends. Thus the alliance has provided firms with a forum for IT exchange and personnel training.

The Alliance for the Joint Development of Notebook Computers is the biggest targeted project for co-operative development among producers of technological products. It combines the resources of three groups of actors – firms, research organizations and unions – in joint co-operation. The greatest achievements of this alliance are that it boosted group strength, completed the development of the central processing unit (CPU) in three months, established technical standards and specifications, produced a prototype,[3] took advantage of computer exhibitions to disseminate information and grasped new market opportunities. The creation of such a critical mass of knowledge has helped Taiwan as a whole become today's biggest manufacturing base for notebook computers in the world.

Subsidies – 'Development Methods for Leading New Products'

In order to encourage privately operated businesses to develop leading new products, thereby stimulating the emerging hi-tech industry, the advancement of the whole industry has been promoted. The Industrial Development Bureau has encouraged manufacturers to create new products by means of 'subsidies for the development of leading new products', aimed at reducing costs and risks borne by SMEs in developing such goods.

In line with this method, all firms producing leading new products complying with the following principles are eligible to apply:

1. The product comes from the emerging hi-tech industry (including communications, information products, consumer electronics, aerospace, medical health care, pollution prevention, high-grade materials, semiconductors, special chemical products and pharmaceuticals, fine mechanic and automation sectors).
2. The product's key technology must be more advanced than current domestic industrial and technical standards.
3. The product has a strong inherent interconnective effect, a large potential market and can promote the development of the relevant industry.

For a development plan of a leading new product that has been examined and approved, 50 per cent of the development costs falling within the scope outlined above are covered by government subsidies.

Venture Capital

In 1984, Taiwan's government planned and established a venture capital fund (VCF), enabling venture capitalists to invest according to their specialized abilities in emerging industries with great development potential. The fund provides capital and administrative assistance and, after the enterprise has developed successfully, also releases holdings for profit. Based on the US experience, the venture capital fund joins unlimited innovative ability of technical inventors to the funds of venture capitalists. By integrating the mutual interests of these two groups of actors, it has stimulated the dramatic growth of technological specialization. As for the technical inventors, unless they develop technology in the research laboratory of a big company, they are required to work as private individuals, minority groups or small companies. Thus the main target of venture capital is either individuals or SMEs. Venture capital is expected to make a valuable contribution to the growth of SMEs, especially in emerging industries.

During its 15 year history, the VCF has grown constantly and it is still playing a dynamic role in promoting the national hi-tech industry. To date, a total of NT$43.5 billion has been invested in 1,839 cases, with an average of NT$23.67 million for each of them. On the whole, the most modern hi-tech manufacturers are SMEs. Since the investment of venture capitalists is concentrated in the hi-tech industry, this has contributed substantially to facilitate the upgrading of specialized SMEs in Taiwan.

Hsinchu Science-based Industrial Park

In order to stimulate investment and technology transfer from high-tech industries, in 1980 the government established a science-based industrial park similar to those established in Silicon Valley. In selecting the location for the new park the availability of suitable manpower and technical support were considered crucial conditions. Hsinchu possessed two universities which were particularly strong in sciences (National Tsinghua University and National Chiao Tung University) and which could ensure that there would be no shortage of highly qualified personnel.   Moreover, as the Industrial Technology Research Institute (ITRI) had been established in Hsinchu to provide general technological support, Hsinchu came up as the obvious choice. The government provided five years of tax exemption for firms willing to locate within the park, along with exemption from import duty, commodity tax and business tax for equipment, raw materials, parts and semi-finished products imported from abroad and a variety of other incentive measures.[4]

The original blueprint for the establishment of the Park was Silicon Valley, the heart of the US electronics industry, and today the Hsinchu Science-based Industrial Park has without question become 'Taiwan's Silicon Valley'. A large number of overseas Chinese have been successfully attracted into the park, whether to establish plants and factories there or to engage in production-supporting or R&D-related activities. This has also given a significant contribution to the improvement of technological levels of related industries in Taiwan. Thus the main additions that the Hsinchu Science-based Industrial Park have made to Taiwan's industrial development have been to effectively introduce overseas technology and to encourage technical experts living overseas to return home. In the 1990s, almost a third of the firms located in the Hsinchu Park had been established by overseas Chinese.

Furthermore, the establishment of the science-based industrial park has also helped the diffusion of technology by encouraging manufacturers to reap the benefits of spatial agglomeration. A questionnaire survey on 390 semiconductor manufacturers located within the park conducted by Mai, Chang and Hsu Yu in 1999 reached two main results:

1. the fluid nature of the labour market for this industry implied that the concentration of manufacturers within the park had positive effects in terms of stimulating informal technical exchange between firms;
2. as far as individual employees were concerned, being able to move between different firms within the same technological area has created a 'boundaryless career', making it possible for employees to keep learning throughout their professional life, as well as to establish a wide network of contacts.

Even more important was the technical network that was established; the clustering of manufacturers in the same area increased the possibility of cross-plant learning, and helped lower the cost of individual employees' turnover.

Currently, the Science-based Industrial Park has become the main centre of development of Taiwan's hi-tech industries. According to the 1997 business volume ranking, the semiconductor industry was the largest industry within the park, followed by computers and computer peripherals, communications, optoelectronics, precision machinery and biochemicals. In 1997 there were 245 companies located in the park, employing a total of 68,410 workers; total business volume accounted for US$13.9 billion and the park's output value accounted for around 5 per cent of the country's total production value.

The inter-organizational linkage and access to the 'Taiwanese Silicon Valley' provided learning-by-doing effects and technology spillovers, a great exposure to the international economy due to OEM/ODM contracts and a strong tie with Chinese born engineers.

Government-sponsored Research Institutes

Government-sponsored institutions serve as intermediate agents for technology transfer. ITRI was established in 1973 as a part of the Ministry of Economic Affairs (MOEA) with government funding, and its major task is to develop technologies and new products related to industrial development, transferring these research results to local firms; consequently, ITRI is an important channel of government intervention in civil R&D. More than 60 per cent of the Science and Technology Project (STP) – with an annual budget of over NT$10 billion – has been, since 1995, under the purview of ITRI. ITRI's most widely recognized contributions to the electronics industry over the last ten years include the following points:

1. first, it constitutes a major channel for technology exchanges. Several areas of generic technology with external benefits have been developed

by ITRI and then diffused to private sector manufacturers with particular attention to SMEs. This has helped increase the technical competitiveness of individual firms, industries and that of Taiwan as a whole. ITRI and other corporate research institutions have played the role of intermediaries in technology transfer and have made an important contribution to raising the technological levels of domestic producers;

2.   ITRI has helped the diffusion of talent, boosting the R&D capability of domestic firms and speeding up the spread of new technology. Skilled technical personnel trained at ITRI – and at its specialized divisions[5] – often join enterprises after leaving the institution, thereby indirectly building and cultivating the R&D capacity of the private sector. Taking the semiconductor industry as an example, a high proportion of the personnel of United Microelectronics Corp. and Taiwan Semiconductor Manufacturing Co. – from their chairmen down to researchers – came from ITRI. Even the production facilities and some of the technology used by these companies were provided by ITRI. The Institute has thus played a major role in creating the success that Taiwan's semiconductor industry enjoys today;

3.   ITRI has helped improve industrial competitiveness through inter-firm collaboration. In order to make science and technology policies conform better to the real needs of the industry, private companies have been encouraged to collaborate on science and technology policies with corporate research institutions. This has become increasingly common since 1991 and has made a significant contribution to the improvement of industrial competitiveness.

The Institute for Information Industry (III), also under the MOEA, was established in 1979 and it is responsible for research related to software, services and computer use, that is later transferred to the domestic software industry. Within the Institute for Information Industry, the Market Intelligence Centre (MIC) provides market research for the computer industry. The Institute for Information Industry has a staff of 1,200 people, 80 per cent of whom are professionals.

7. FUTURE CHALLENGES FOR TAIWAN'S SMES

New Business Opportunities

There are several potential business opportunities for SMEs to be explored in the future, as the spreading popularity of Internet and multimedia applications are dramatically changing the information industry. Just to mention the most commonly discussed nowadays in Taiwan:

1. the use of various generations of Pentium CPUs in recently developed PCs, combined with the increasing scale of multimedia applications, will substantially raise the demand for multimedia products, to the benefit of multimedia manufacturers and multimedia IC design houses;
2. the need for users to constantly upgrade Internet access hardware in order to avoid costly time delays will give impetus to data networking, network IC manufacturing and network software engineering, offering further business opportunities for SMEs in related areas;
3. the Internet can be conceptualized as a tool for reducing transaction costs. For instance, on the retail side, the external costs associated with opening, maintaining and staffing physical stores are reduced. On the production/distribution side, generation and circulation of paper has strongly diminished. Start-up costs are also greatly squeezed by the Internet, as well as the costs of intermediate inputs' provision and inventory management. This has led to a proliferation of individuals and firms attempting to use the Web for commercial purposes. All these represent additional potential business opportunities for SMEs.

Internal Threats

Despite the emerging business opportunities, at least two inherent weaknesses threaten the future of Taiwanese SMEs in high-tech sectors. First, because of their small scale, SMEs lack management resources, such as R&D capability and human resources for future planning. Second, close networks sometimes hinder SMEs in the process of upgrading; a single firm cannot undertake the upgrading of its technology on the basis of an individual effort, as it has to take into account the contributions of many subcontractors and co-ordinate the upgrading throughout the whole network.

Nonetheless, profit margins for computer hardware are thin for companies that do not control critical technologies. Taiwan needs to continue to improve its technological capabilities and develop strategies – such as original design manufacturing (ODM) – in order to stay competitive. Survival as an OEM can nowadays be precarious, as customers can always look for cheaper suppliers. Taiwan's shift to a full-service OEM/ODM producer has bolstered its position in the market. Eventually, an increasing number of companies may decide to follow the strategy of Acer (the leading firm in Taiwan's PC industry) in developing their own brand-name products for export. The creation of brand-names is rather expensive,[6] but it allows firms to control their distribution channels and generate demand from end users. In addition to hardware production, a concerted effort in software and related information services to strengthen domestic capabilities and investments in the production of key components – such as LCD panels, batteries and DRAMs – to enhance product value-added are urgently needed.

In general, SMEs with flexible production and management efficiency are better equipped to cope with the rapidly changing technological environment. Lai's (1998) empirical analysis indicates that the rapid growth of Taiwan's electronics industry in the period 1986-92 was mainly accounted for by the huge number of established SMEs that had higher management efficiency than large firms.

External Challenges

Taiwan's SMEs also face a challenge from unfavourable changes in the external environment. SMEs' overall share of manufacturing sales has been decreasing steadily since the late 1980s and their share of sales in electronics fell slightly in the second half of the 1990s. This trend might indicate that the environment for Taiwan's OEM/ODM-dominated economy is changing. The proliferation of low-priced PCs may significantly affect SMEs.

Global PC suppliers (such as IBM, Compaq and Dell) have adopted a so-called Build to Order (BTO) strategy in order to maintain their profit margins with the proliferation of low-priced computers. Under the original OEM contract system, OEM manufactures (for example Taiwanese firms such as Acer and Mitac) would project PC demand for the next three or four months and then ship these units to global PC vendors (such as IBM and Compaq). These latter companies controlled shipment to distributors (customers), inventory management and related costs. Under the BTO system, instead, marketing agents (distributors) report demand for PCs to global PC vendors, which in turn place orders with OEM manufacturers. The OEM manufacturers must deliver the PCs to their own overseas warehouses or operation bases located near the global PC vendors' customers (distributors) within two or three weeks. In a sense, under the BTO system global PC vendors delegate responsibility for shipment, inventory control, financial leverage, components and raw materials preparation to the OEM manufacturers.

The differences between the BTO model and the original PC shipment model are summarized in Figure 4.5.

The BTO system has several implications. First, big firms may 'swallow-up' small firms. Those smaller OEM manufacturers that do not develop a global logistic ability will be forced to pursue niche markets or to become regional suppliers. Second, profit margins of component suppliers will be under heavy pressure as the global PC vendors squeeze every last penny out of the OEM manufacturers, which in turn undercut the prices of their

Original PC shipment model

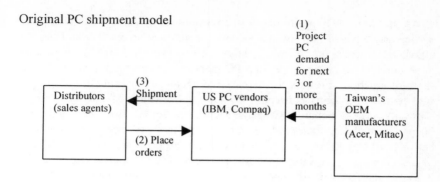

BTO model

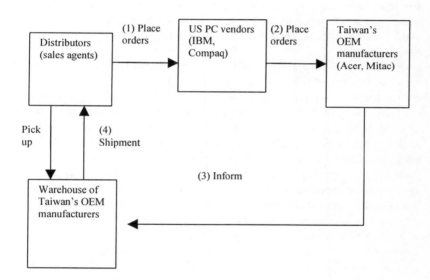

Figure 4.5 Differences between the BTO model and the original PC shipment model

components suppliers in order to maintain their own profit margins. Third, fiercer price competition will bring down corporate profits and, as a consequence, firms without good management may be driven out of the market. Particularly during periods of currency crisis, price-cutting strategies are bound to become popular with OEM manufacturers to enable them to gain market shares or to survive in the market. In such circumstances, lower prices and reduced sales will translate into lower corporate profits.

As low-price PCs proliferate, the environment for SMEs could become particularly adverse in Taiwan's electronics industry, given its emphasis on OEM/ODM production. First, the largest seven firms account for more than three-quarters of Taiwan's desktop-PC market. Second, the top seven firms' share of notebook-PC exports increased to about 10 per cent (from 78.6 per cent to 87.3 per cent) between 1997 and 1998. Third, of the 70 firms in Taiwan's SME-dominated IC design sector, the top ten firms accounted for 90 per cent of total sales. Moreover, the top three IC design houses hold between 40 and 50 per cent of the market and all three are actually affiliates of large enterprises. Furthermore, as Lee and Yu (1996) pointed out, although in traditional industrial sectors – such as, for example, textiles and clothing – the division of labour was balanced between large enterprises and SMEs, this is not the case in high-tech sectors. Large enterprises can always use their stronger bargaining power to switch OEM contracts. This adds to the traditional weaknesses of SMEs relative to large enterprises in recruiting skilled technical personnel and obtaining other production factors such as land and capital.

Taiwan's computer industry was built around small, nimble and medium-sized enterprises which could get to the market faster than the giants that dominated the industry in Japan and Korea. The PC industry has recently evolved to a point, however, where economies of scale are critical to success. Only large producers can get volume discounts on components, or offer the scale of production necessary to handle major OEM accounts. The same situation holds for components and peripherals such as motherboards and monitors. The result of this is that the industry is consolidating, with the top five producers accounting for the large majority of most product categories. Some SMEs have grown into relatively large companies and have come to dominate certain market segments.

In addition, the growing capital requirements and the technological complexity that accompanied the rapid industrial transformation of the island produced new forms of business organization (Ernst, 1997a). When electronics took over textiles and clothing as the leading industrial sector, this led to an erosion of Taiwan's traditional form of business organization: SMEs owned by loose family networks.

Thus the trend in the high-tech industry seems to move towards oligopoly and against SMEs. There are only very limited areas in the high-tech manufacturing industry – such as IC-design, software and information services – where SMEs can play a crucial role in the future. In other areas, SMEs will need to become OEM partners of large firms or regional suppliers in a niche market.

8. CONCLUSIONS

In this chapter some empirical evidence on the development of SMEs in Taiwan has been briefly described. In particular, following the decline of the textile and clothing exports to the advantage of electronics, the growth of the latter industry has been characterized by a significant change of product composition. Consumer electronics and home appliances have been replaced by information and communication products, while integrated circuits have taken a growing share of the electronic components sector. The more labour-intensive, low-technology products have been either wiped out by foreign competition or have had to be transferred to overseas production bases in China and South-east Asia. Only sectors with high capital and technology intensity could survive. As a result, the role of SMEs has slightly decreased but, due to the rapidly changing technological environment, there are still great opportunities for SMEs to work on new aspects of technology, to discover different applications and to produce better quality components or products to confirm and strengthen their position in the international market.

Taiwan's electronics industry (as in the case of the labour-intensive textiles and clothing) has heavily relied on OEM production. Indeed, by concentrating on production and leaving marketing and other activities to multinationals, Taiwanese SMEs have acquired a strong position in the global competitive market. The flexible, highly specialized and co-operative production networks helped SMEs produce efficiently. However, given the competitive nature of the market, those who failed to meet the new challenges were wiped out from the scene. Only those who successfully upgraded their technologies and enhanced production efficiency managed to survive and grow. Constant challenge from mighty Korean conglomerates and firms from other emerging Asian countries forced Taiwan's SMEs to search all the time for new products and new market niches and to improve their production efficiency and technological capability.

This ongoing challenge-and-response process further strengthened Taiwan's co-operative production networks. Currently facing harsher competitive pressure, firms desperately try to squeeze their input suppliers to cut down costs. Accordingly, input suppliers have to find ways to reduce costs as well, and have to search for cheaper materials and machinery. This means that both downstream and upstream firms should work in tight co-operation to cope with the more aggressive competition. As Taiwanese centre firms are not bounded to buy from their close satellite firms, they can always purchase materials or components from the most competitive sources, enhancing greatly their flexibility. On the other hand, input suppliers have to find ways to safeguard markets and their experiences are commonly used by Taiwanese firms to win over foreign orders.

One very peculiar characteristic of Taiwan's SMEs is that many of them, both in traditional and high-tech industries, have grown into medium-sized or large firms. Successful SMEs usually have ambitions to grow larger: moreover, the increased competitiveness of the financial market and the emerging venture capital have helped speed up SMEs' expansion.

Notwithstanding all their achievements and successes, Taiwanese SMEs are presently facing tough, new challenges. Because of higher labour costs in Taiwan, more and more firms are shifting their production base to China to utilize cheap labour resources available there. Although many remaining firms have still been able to upgrade their technologies and find new market niches so far, it is becoming increasingly difficult to move up the ladder since Taiwanese firms are now competing with the best firms from all over the world in highly advanced productions. The need for more capital-intensive and R&D-intensive activities makes it rather difficult for SMEs to survive and grow. Pursuing diversified applications and designs may constitute a successful strategy, but how to market the designed products is still a big challenge for Taiwan's SMEs. Furthermore, as the competitiveness of mainland China is becoming stronger – also with the help of Taiwanese direct investment – SMEs in the small economy are increasingly jeopardized.

On the issue of industrial agglomeration, the evidence from Taiwan's industrial development is mixed. Contrary to the case of the textile and clothing industry – for which there are several clusters more precisely identifiable – it is not so clear to what extent agglomeration in a narrow sense has been an important factor for industrial development in the electronic industry, in spite of the evidence that some kind of geographical concentration exists for each sector in the industry. For example, the set-up of export processing zones in Koahsiung City and the science park in Hsinchu County did provide crucial infrastructures and services for SMEs' growth. On the other hand, however, there is no evidence that the firms located inside the park perform better than those outside. Indeed, personal networking between engineering and technical staff, natural just-in-time (JIT) or near-JIT delivery cycles, ample second sources in the event of supply shortage and immediate engineering and technical support may be better explained on the basis of the small size of the country as a whole, rather than by clustering in specific locations.

How to preserve and make competitive small business operations, and how to effectively perpetuate the division of labour between SMEs and large enterprises in the global production networks, are pressing issues at stake for the Taiwanese government.

NOTES

1. See Chapter 5 in this volume.
2. In this section, data collected from the censuses of 1986, 1991 and 1996 are reported to give a picture of the weight of SMEs and their geographical distribution. The census data provided by the Directorate General of Budget of the Executive Yuan of Taiwan constitute by far the most comprehensive and accurate economic data set, although the survey is conducted only once every five years and the categorization of industries may change for different census periods, creating problems of comparison.
3. In June 1990, the alliance invested over 14,000 person-hours in completing a computer prototype, which, however, could only be produced in small quantities.
4. See Liu (1993, pp. 306-7). These include low-interest loans, the right to retain earnings of up to 200 per cent of paid-in-capital, a five-year income tax holiday within the first nine years of operation, accelerating depreciation of R&D equipment and low-cost land.
5. Two such divisions have played a critical role for the development of Taiwan's computer industry: the Electronic Research Service Organization (ERSO) that has focused on the development of key components (especially ICs and LCDs); and the Computer and Communications Research Laboratories (CCL) that focuses on the development of new architectural designs for computers, communications and consumer electronics.
6. See Chapter 5 in this volume.

5. Small Firms Competing in Globalized High-tech Industries: The Co-evolution of Domestic and International Knowledge Linkages in Taiwan's Computer Industry

Dieter Ernst

---

1. INTRODUCTION

Over the last decade Taiwan has established itself as a world-class supply source for a variety of electronic hardware products. It is the world's largest supplier of computer monitors, motherboards, switching power supplies, mouse devices, keyboards, scanners and a variety of add-on cards. In 1996, almost 60 per cent of the world's desktop PCs were either made in Taiwan or contained a motherboard made by a Taiwanese company;[1] moreover, since 1994 Taiwan has also become the world's largest manufacturer of notebook PCs.

Progress has been equally impressive in the field of electronic components. Taiwan today has hundreds of passive component makers that have established a strong position relative to leading Japanese and US competitors. Taiwanese firms have also improved their position in the capital-intensive mass production of precision components, such as large-scale CRT picture tubes for computer monitors and sophisticated display devices (like active-matrix TFT-LCDs) for laptop computers. The same is true for integrated circuits (ICs).

Two recent structural changes show how Taiwanese firms have upgraded their capabilities: a rapid diversification beyond hard core PC-related products; and a shift from stand-alone manufacturing services to *integrated service packages* that cover a wide range of value chain activities, including higher value-added support services. Taiwanese computer companies now have established themselves as competitive suppliers in a variety of complementary, high-growth market segments, some of which display considerably higher profit margins. Such diversification is evident in three areas: the development of so-called PC network products,[2] especially modems and network interface cards; multimedia accessories, such as CD-ROM drives and add-on cards, and a variety of information services industries, such as multimedia software, system integration, turnkey systems and network services. Most of these information services owe their existence to the convergence of previously separated technologies used for computing, communicating and digital consumer applications, and require the capacity to combine various strands of technology to generate new applications and markets.

Taiwanese firms have also developed a capacity to provide a package of services across a wide range of value chain activities, sustaining their position as preferred OEM (original equipment manufacturing) suppliers to the industry. With the exception of R&D and marketing, practically all other stages of the value chain can now be performed by Taiwan's OEM contractors. Moreover, Taiwanese firms are beginning to shoulder essential co-ordination functions for the *global supply chain* management of their OEM customers.

Taiwan's achievements would be impressive for any country; they are even more impressive for a small island, about one-third the size of New York State. With a population of about 21 million people, roughly half the size of South Korea, Taiwan lacked a large and sophisticated domestic market, specialized capabilities and support industries, and the science and technology infrastructure necessary for developing a broad set of electronics products. From the outset, Taiwan's PC industry depended heavily on international markets and access to foreign technology. Penetrating foreign markets and absorbing imported technology, however, requires conscious efforts to develop a variety of domestic resources and capabilities through deliberate knowledge creation management.[3] How do small enterprises develop such capabilities?

This chapter is divided into six sections. Section 2 describes the dominance of SMEs and their role as a source of flexibility; it also briefly sketches the kind of policy approach that has enabled small Taiwanese firms to get on to the virtuous circle of co-evolving domestic and international knowledge creation linkages. The rest of the chapter (sections 3 to 5) inquires into how inter-organizational knowledge creation has benefited from a variety of linkages with large domestic and foreign firms; some industrial upgrading requirements that result from this peculiar type of knowledge creation are also addressed. Finally, section 6 offers some concluding remarks on the chapter's main findings.

2. THE DOMINANCE OF SMEs

Small and medium-sized enterprises (SMEs) have been the main carriers of Taiwan's rapid development and remain important today. The role of SMEs as engines of growth and industrial transformation sets Taiwan apart from South Korea, where huge and highly diversified conglomerates (*chaebols*), have been the main carriers of the development of the electronics industry (Ernst, 1994a and 1998). Almost without exception, the chaebols have targeted those segments of the electronics industry that require huge investment outlays and sophisticated mass production techniques for fairly homogeneous products like microwave ovens, TV sets, VCRs, computer monitors, picture tubes and computer memories, especially DRAMs. The result has been a heavy focus on assembly-type mass production activities related to lower-end consumer products and standard electronic components, and a weakness in more design-intensive sectors of the computer industry.

Why did Taiwanese firms succeed in the computer industry, while their much larger and resource-rich Korean counterparts have largely failed? The answer lies in the fundamental characteristics of an industry in which high volatility and uncertainty put a premium on flexibility and the capacity to adjust to abrupt and frequently unexpected changes in demand and technology; small firm size can foster such flexibility.[4] By combining incremental product innovation with incredibly fast speed-to-market, Taiwanese firms have been able to establish a strong international market position relatively early in the product cycle.

The primary source of this flexibility appears to be the specific organization of the domestic supply base in Taiwan, especially for parts and components. Two main features of this domestic supply base have contributed to the flexibility of Taiwanese producers, the first being an extreme form of specialization. By engaging in single tasks and by producing, purchasing and selling in small lots, subcontractors avoid heavy fixed capital costs. This in turn makes it relatively easy to shift production at relatively short notice and with a minimum of costs. The second feature is a certain network structure of multiple, volatile and short-term links that involve only limited financial and technology transfers. Spot-market transactions play an important role, but so do 'temporary spider web' arrangements that are assembled for the duration of a particular job.[5] The result of these characteristics is an extreme form of open and volatile production networks, arguably even more so than the highly flexible production networks that characterize California's Silicon Valley.[6] Firms maximize the number of jobs in order to compensate for the razor-thin profit margins; as a result, they avoid being locked into a particular production network. Domestic supplier networks thus have been highly *flexible and capable of rapid change*, but *short-lived and footloose*.

If flexibility constitutes one prerequisite for Taiwan's competitive success in computers, economies of scale and scope and speed-to-market have been of equal importance.[7] Entry barriers have increased for those stages of the value chain which are of critical importance for competitive success, including particularly component manufacturing where production-related scale economies remain important. But the epicentre of competition has shifted beyond manufacturing to R&D and other forms of intangible investment required to complement price competition with product differentiation and speed-to-market. Only those companies can survive that are able to get the right product to the highest volume segment of the market at the right time. Being late is a disaster and often forces companies out of business.

In sum, what really matters for competitive success are substantial investments in the formation of a *firm's technological and organizational capabilities*. How were Taiwanese computer companies able to successfully compete in an industry where size-related advantages are of critical importance? And, more specifically, what kind of organizational innovations have enabled Taiwanese firms to overcome their size-related disadvantages?

In order to answer these questions, we need to examine the issues of *specialization and co-ordination*. Andersen (1996) has recently provided an interesting theoretical explanation why excessive specialization may involve substantial trade-offs. He shows that, as an economy becomes more specialized, this increases the pressure for standardization. In turn, this may constrain innovation.[8] The solution to this dilemma is the establishment of tight linkages between firms along the supply chain that enhance the prospects for inter-organizational knowledge creation, for instance between end product manufacturers and component suppliers.[9] To understand how Taiwan avoided the dangers of excessive specialization and established tight inter-firm linkages, it is important to correct some popular misconceptions of the Taiwanese model. This is not an economy characterized by *atomistic* competition. SMEs do play an important role, yet they survive due to a combination of four forces: government policies that facilitated market entry and upgrading; strong linkages with large Taiwanese firms and business groups; the presence of foreign sales and manufacturing affiliates; and early participation in international production networks.

As far as the first factor is concerned, though Korea and Taiwan share many similarities, the two countries have chosen very different policy approaches. In the early 1960s the Taiwanese government introduced aggressive programmes to encourage investment by domestic as well as foreign companies.[10] In line with similar programmes in Korea, these statutes provided generous tax incentives and laid down rules to facilitate the acquisition of land for industrial use by investors and access to utilities. Five features, however, distinguished Taiwan's approach.

First, no limits were set on the number of firms within each industry group, with the exception of a few mining and utility industries. Any domestic firm could invest and enjoy the same tax and other privileges. This open policy gave rise to intense domestic competition, and was conducive to a *diversified* industry structure. Second, the government actively promoted the development and modernization of Taiwan's SME sector. The first of such policies, 'The Rule for Promotion of Small and Medium Enterprises', was promulgated in 1967 and was subsequently revised several times as Taiwan's SMEs grew. Government assistance to SMEs included market promotion, management rationalization, co-operation and promoting strategic alliances, loans and upgrading technology and labour training (Ministry of Economic Affairs (MOEA), 1991). Third, there was no discrimination against smaller firms *within* the SME category. Any firm, irrespective of size, could participate and was treated equally. This *neutral* policy was an important foundation for the development of Taiwan's large pool of vibrant and entrepreneurial SMEs. Fourth, virtually equal treatment was granted to domestic and foreign investment, with the exception of some majority share-holding regulations applicable to foreign firms and strict foreign exchange control regulations governing domestic firms. This balanced policy attracted foreign investment without producing the 'crowding-out' that occurred in Singapore, where domestic firms have played a minimal role in the manufacturing sector.[11]

Finally, an important difference that sets apart Taiwan's industrial policies from those pursued in Korea is that directed credit has played a much less important role, at least until the early 1980s. This can be seen from the high real interest rates for secured loans that Taiwanese firms had to pay during this period.[12] This has changed only since the mid-1980s, when the focus of industrial policy shifted to industrial upgrading. Any firm, irrespective of size, could participate in industrial promotion programmes, including concessionary credit. In contrast to the Korean government, which used its control of the finance sector to direct credit to a handful of chaebols, *the Taiwanese government did not try to promote large national champions.* One should also mention that curb markets have arguably played a more important role in Taiwan than in Korea as an alternative source of debt finance relative to bank credit. The result is that Taiwan's corporate debt-equity ratio is substantially lower than in Korea:[13] Taiwan's net debt-equity ratio for 1998 is forecast to be around 30 per cent, compared with more than 180 per cent for Korea.[14]

Differences in industrial policy have led to very different firm behaviour in the Korean and in the Taiwanese electronics industries. Arguably, some of these differences explain why Taiwan has been less vulnerable than Korea to the impact of the financial crisis (Ernst, 1998). Taiwan's industrial policy is focused on competition: relatively low entry barriers and non-discriminatory policies enable small firms to enter targeted sectors and to grow. At the same time the legal system puts relatively few obstacles in the way of bankruptcy. This has forced incumbents to stay trim; they have also accelerated the spread of information, skills and knowledge. The result is that Taiwan's smaller companies had to rely more on equity markets and corporate retained earnings than the chaebol: Taiwanese firms find it more difficult to raise capital for large-scale volume production and they are under much greater pressure to submit investment decisions to short-term financial considerations.

In sum, Taiwan's development strategy generated forward and backward linkage effects, while relying on 'market-augmenting' policies that reduced risk and uncertainty rather than market-repressing policies that increased fragmentation and rent-seeking (Johnson, 1987, p. 141). Taiwan's policy approach was not a static one, however, as the requirements of industrial upgrading changed over time, so did the nature of state intervention. This *continuous upgrading* of industrial policies has been an important defining element of Taiwan's approach to knowledge creation.[15]

Policy requirements keep changing over time for two simple reasons: increasing complexity and a greater exposure to the international economy. As Taiwan's industry moves up from simple and labour-intensive to more complex products, much more sophisticated policies are required. The main reason is that *entry barriers rise with increasing complexity*: investment thresholds increase and knowledge requirements become more demanding. For small enterprises this implies that they need to have access to *externalities* that would enable them to overcome their size-related disadvantages.[16] A *greater exposure to the international economy* is a second reason why industrial development policies need to develop over time. An increasing complexity of the domestic industry necessitates more international linkages. Such linkages are necessary to facilitate local capability formation; they do not only encompass critical imports of key components and capital equipment and inward FDI. Such linkages also involve participation in global production networks (GPNs) as well as in a variety of specialized and informal 'international peer group' networks that are essential carriers of knowledge creation, especially in the computer industry. Left on their own, small enterprises are ill-equipped to reap the benefits of such international linkages. Again, the market needs to be complemented by selective policy interventions that can provide some of the necessary externalities.

3. THE ROLE OF INTER-ORGANIZATIONAL LINKAGES

We have seen that small, family-owned firms have played an important role in the development of Taiwan's electronics industry. This had considerable advantages, both in terms of cost and flexibility: transaction costs were low, as family-run enterprises co-operated on the basis of informal social contacts. Outsourcing could be performed at much lower cost, risks could be substantially reduced and information circulated much more quickly.

This type of arrangement is now coming under increasing pressure, and appears to be ill-equipped to deal with the new competitive requirements. Family bonds erode, especially when the firm has to move production overseas and loose networks between family-owned SMEs are unable to raise the capital required for increasing fixed investments and R&D outlays. As a result, Taiwanese SMEs had to develop a variety of linkages with more powerful third parties.

It is difficult to say which of these different linkage arrangements are most effective to cope with the dual challenge of knowledge creation and internationalization. We find that Taiwanese SMEs, as well as the government, have pursued a *plurality* of approaches in parallel, rather than concentrating exclusively on one particular linkage.

Informal 'Peer Group' Networks

Taiwanese SMEs have always relied heavily on *informal social networks* for access to resources, capabilities and knowledge that they are unable to mobilize on their own. Over time, the focus of these networks has shifted from labour, capital and basic market information to technological knowledge and brand name recognition. Originally these networks were restricted to family and kinship relations. They are now rapidly being substituted by professional 'peer group' networks. This is especially true for the electronics industry where resource and capability requirements are much more demanding than in traditional industries, and where participation in international knowledge networks is of the essence.

Informal peer group networks come in a variety of forms. Typically, classmates (especially in elite schools) and former colleagues (especially in foreign affiliates) form tight networks that can be instrumental in the creation of start-up companies. For example, Taiwanese SMEs rely heavily on informal information exchange with former classmates for the generation of tacit knowledge on specific engineering and marketing problems and when they need confidential information on potential partners or competitors. Interviews at Acer for instance showed that even today, when this company has long moved beyond its earlier SME status, senior managers still prefer to contact former teachers or classmates when they have to deal with a specific engineering, marketing or management problem rather than a commercial consultancy firm or a technology research institute.

Acer actually has been a master in the formation of such informal networks; much of its success is arguably due to the scope and depth of its peer group linkages. Founded in 1976 as Multitech International Corp., with a registered capital of just $25,000 and 11 employees, the company's first activity was to run a training centre for computer engineers. In the first three years more than 3,000 engineers were trained who later were to occupy important positions in Taiwan's nascent computer industry. As a result, Acer was able to establish early on an extensive network of social contacts within Taiwan's computer community. These contacts have become an important asset. Since 1986 Acer Sertek Inc., the company's domestic sales, marketing and service arm, has trained more than 170,000 Taiwanese students in computer use.[17]

A Hierarchical Centre-Satellite System and Institutional Innovations for Internationalization

Another attempt to overcome the disadvantages of small firm size has been the government's *Centre-Satellite Programme* (CS), launched in 1984, in response to the private sector's reluctance to vertically integrate production through either merger or inter-firm co-operation. The objective of this programme has been to eliminate cut-throat competition and destructive price cutting practices by encouraging closer, interdependent and long-term ties between larger 'centre' firms (upstream suppliers, final assemblers, large trading companies) and their 'satellites' (especially component suppliers). In order to strengthen these links, the government provides a variety of financial, manpower training and technical engineering assistance to both the central plants and the satellites.

Most assessments conclude that the CS programme so far has only been partially successful (San Gee, 1995a and Wade, 1990, p. 167). Yet these assessments need to be placed in a broader context. Over the last few years the CS programme has generated an increasing variety of linkages between SMEs and large firms, linkages that frequently extend beyond national boundaries. Government policies to promote CS networks were particularly successful in accelerating the outward investment of SMEs to Southeast Asia and China. Once a foreign lead company of an OEM network had invested in these regions, this exerted a powerful pressure on Taiwanese satellites to follow suit and to move their production offshore. In many cases this has had the unanticipated effect of 'hollowing-out' the domestic supplier system. In order to correct and avoid such negative impacts, both government policies and firm strategies are currently being adjusted. Government policies now pay more attention to assisting SMEs to upgrade their domestic activities. This applies especially to incentives for technology diffusion and product-related R&D; incentives for training; policies to improve infrastructure and access to telecommunications services: and policies to improve financial services. For their part, firms are striving to diversify and internationalize their ownership, and to reap broader benefits from international specialization and the building of proprietary assets.

Industrial parks and, later on, science parks played a major role in the development of Taiwan's locational advantages. This organizational innovation is now being transferred abroad, especially to the southern coastal provinces of China and Southeast Asia. Over the last few years there has been a rapid proliferation of special business zones and industrial estates that are geared primarily to the needs of Taiwanese small and medium-sized computer companies. The original role models are the 'shoe city' and the 'textile city' established in the southern coastal Chinese province of Fujian. This has been followed by similar arrangements in the electronics industry, such as two 'Cities of Electronics' (in Fujian and Guangdong provinces of China), the Penang Scientific Park in Malaysia, the Kung-Hua Industrial Park on Batan Island (Indonesia) and the Subic Bay Industrial Park in the Philippines.

Since the Taiwanese government cannot openly act as a third party, for political reasons, a variety of intermediary institutional approaches provide similar services. The largest project so far has been the conversion of Subic Bay, the former US naval base in the Philippines, into a major industrial park, primarily for Taiwanese and American electronic firms. The idea is to enable Taiwanese subcontractors to move jointly with their large Taiwanese lead contractors and major American OEM clients. The provision of low-interest loans by the International Economic Co-operation and Development Fund (IECDF), Taiwan's foreign aid programme, is designed to help Taiwanese SMEs to invest in Subic Bay and other neighbouring locations. The goal is to transfer parts of the domestic Taiwanese supply base for components and sub-assemblies to Southeast Assa, so that final assemblers of monitors, motherboards and PCs and other PC-related products can have access on the spot to low-cost and flexible support industries.

At the same time this creates new mechanisms for inter-organizational knowledge creation. Take the case of Advanced Semiconductor Engineering Inc. (ASE), the world's second largest independent contract assembler of ICs, which already has a plant in Penang, Malaysia, to supplement its parent facility in Kaohsiung. ASE now wants to expand in Subic Bay as well. The company already uses Philippine workers in Kaohsiung and has given them intensive training. Since the Taiwanese government allows foreign workers to work in Taiwan for two years only, ASE will send them to Subic Bay as trainers of its workforce there.

Linkages with Large Domestic Firms: Cross-sectoral Business Groups

Contrary to conventional wisdom, *large firms have played a central role in the co-ordination and development of the Taiwanese production system*. They have also facilitated knowledge creation in small firms. After the Second World War the Taiwanese government took over the Japanese enterprises that had been established during the 50 years of colonial rule (1895-1945). In contrast to Korea, the government did not privatize these firms: instead they were run as public enterprises. By developing *a strong public enterprise sector*, Taiwan developed companies large enough to enter the highly capital-intensive production of basic materials, while at the same time avoiding the dominance of private conglomerates (San Gee and Wen-jeng Kuo, 1998; Schive, 1990).

Linkages with large firms have played an important role in the development of Taiwan's SME sector. To start with, SMEs depend on the supply of basic materials provided by large public enterprises at low cost and high quality (Wade, 1990). Large firms have also acted as an important intermediary source of capital for SMEs. Taiwan's banks direct most of their funds to large domestic public and private firms who then on-lend money for equipment and working capital to smaller customers, subcontractors and suppliers at higher rates through trade credit and loans on the informal curb market (MOEA, 1991).

It is important to emphasize that many SMEs are for all practical purposes members of a particular business group.[18] The growing capital requirements and technological complexity that accompanied the rapid industrial transformation of the island produced new forms of business organization. When electronics took over from textiles as the leading industrial sector, this led to an erosion of Taiwan's traditional form of business organization: the loose networks of family-owned SMEs (Kuo and Wang, Chapter 4 in this volume). In order to retain profitability, family firms were forced to venture across product lines and to move from industries with declining margins, like textiles, to the much more profitable electronics sector. In most cases, however, they were unable to raise the capital required for increasing fixed investment and R&D: as late as 1992, only 20 per cent of a sample of Taiwanese manufacturing firms were engaged in R&D.[19]

Attempts to cope with these two conflicting pressures produced a peculiar Taiwanese form of business organization: *cross-sectoral business groups*. These business groups are very different from the large, hierarchical *chaebols* that are typical of South Korea, but they also differ from the *keiretsu* system that has dominated much of Japan's industry. In Taiwan, business groups typically consist of a loose network of mostly medium-sized companies that produce a variety of products for different markets, with one core company exercising financial control. This type of firm organization reflects the need to combine the scale advantages of large firms with the speed and flexibility of smaller firms.

The ADI business group provides a typical example. Founded in 1979, the company is run by the Liao Jian-cheng family. From trading and construction it first moved into shoe manufacturing for international mass merchandisers. Around the mid-1980s the family decided to move into electronics. The breakthrough came in 1993, thanks to big orders from Compaq. Despite success in computer monitors, the owners maintain their diversification strategy. ADI has continued to expand its position in shoe manufacturing while at the same time investing in a number of new small start-up companies in software, system design, and in a variety of unrelated commercial activities.

The shift to business groups has been most pronounced in the electronics industry. This is hardly surprising, given the critical importance of economies of scale and scope in this industry. But in the Taiwanese case there are two additional reasons why SMEs became integrated into larger business groups: linkages with foreign customers through international subcontracting and OEM arrangements; and linkages with international supply sources, especially for key components. As a result of these linkages, size became essential to secure economies of scale and scope and achieve sufficient bargaining clout with foreign customers and suppliers. In order to fulfil an OEM contract, large Taiwanese companies like Tatung, First International Computer (which is part of the Formosa Plastics group), Mitac and Acer rely on hundreds of loosely affiliated domestic suppliers to which they can pass on an endless variety of low-margin, yet quite demanding manufacturing and design tasks. The typical Taiwanese small computer company thus often gets involved with foreign firms only in an *indirect* way; large Taiwanese business groups dominate the direct interface with foreign customers. The same is true for the affiliates of foreign multinationals like Philips, Matsushita, DEC and others that have substantial production platforms in Taiwan (see also Kuo and Wang, Chapter 4 in this volume).

A similar mechanism also works on the *procurement* side, especially for high-end key components like DRAMs, microprocessors, CRT picture tubes for computer monitors and liquid crystal displays (LCDs) for laptop computers. The insecurity of supply plays an important role in the formation of inter-firm linkages. Roughly 85 per cent of all semiconductors used in Taiwan are currently imported. Under 'normal' circumstances, Taiwanese SMEs rely on the 'spot market': they purchase these components from the branch offices or agents of foreign component vendors. But normal circumstances are rare in these component markets. When a serious component supply shortage occurs Taiwanese SMEs will be the worst hit. Foreign vendors will either require sharp price mark-ups or refuse to deliver.

For SMEs, the only hope is to survive in the shadow of the large Taiwanese PC manufacturers. During a typical supply shortage, the large Taiwanese manufacturers will expand their procurement orders well beyond their real needs. By buying large quantities of components before price wars actually materialize, firms seek to buffer their effects; one could call this the '*component future trading*' effect. Firms also seek to hedge against opportunism on the part of foreign suppliers. Major Taiwanese PC companies simply must keep large safety inventories of key components as a risk minimization strategy. Third, during shortages, foreign component suppliers normally only supply their strategic customers. For Taiwanese PC makers it is of critical importance to get on such 'strategic customer' lists. The way to do this is to inflate their component orders above their real needs to convince foreign suppliers that the Taiwanese customers are big and important. As a result of these purchasing strategies, Taiwanese PC makers regularly get bogged down with large inventories of key components. The product composition of these inventories keeps rapidly changing, with newer component generations vying for precious inventory space with older ones. Taiwanese PC makers are thus under strong pressure to re-sell parts of their component inventories to local SMEs. Most of these re-sales are components that are 'one generation behind the leading edge'. Prices charged are higher than the prices paid by the large PC maker to the foreign supplier, but lower than those charged on the spot market.[20]

Over the last few years the importance of big business groups has further increased, blurring the division between small and large firms. Taiwan's electronics industry has recently witnessed a rapid increase of concentration. In the PC industry the top ten firms today control roughly 80 per cent of total production, and some of the most powerful Taiwanese business groups (Formosa Plastics, HwaHsin, China Steel, YFY Paper) have now also entered the production of key components, like DRAMs, CRTs and displays.

Business Groups Centred around a Holding Company

Many Taiwanese computer companies have experienced very rapid growth since the last industry shake-out in 1992; the challenge now is to develop an organization that enables them to improve *organizational learning*. For PC manufacturers, the main role model is the *client-server model*. A rapidly growing company like Acer or Mitac spins business units into independent profit centres, creating a *federation of loosely connected companies* united by four factors: access to *common core technologies*; access to the holding company's *financial resources*; access to its *knowledge base, market intelligence and technology scanning capabilities*; and a *common brand name*. This type of organizational innovation makes it possible to keep high value-added operations and core capabilities in Taiwan, while dispersing sales, marketing, procurement, product integration and service operations around the world, in close proximity to the main growth markets.

Each of the different members of a 'client-server organization' are separated by product lines and by geographic region, and each operates independently from the other. This allows them to make decisions quickly in response to market changes and to define the market segments where they feel fit for leadership. At the same time, however, all of these businesses have ready access to the lead company's knowledge base.

One important element of this re-organization is a new approach to overseas PC assembly. Acer provides an example.[21] In order to reduce cost and increase speed-to-market for new products, Acer has established 15 modular assembly sites around the world. Each of these assembly subsidiaries is located close to important markets and performs only very limited activities: it receives PC housings and floppy disk drives by sea, with motherboards flown in directly to ensure delivery of the newest technologies. Central processing units (CPUs), hard drives and memory are sourced locally to fill individual user requirements, and the modular components are assembled quickly according to a standardized procedure. This strategy allows Acer to maintain control over product quality and keep inventory to a minimum, while providing fast assembly of competitively priced PCs that always contain the latest microprocessor generation.

The Taiwanese 'client-server' model comes strikingly close to the basic philosophy of many proponents of corporate re-engineering, especially the model that IBM's previous chairman John Akers had tried to implement for the ailing giant before he was ousted.[22] Yet the basic motivation of firms like Acer has been fundamentally different from that of IBM; the goal is not to reduce the cost of excessive centralization, but *to overcome some size-related barriers to knowledge creation and internationalization*, without repeating the mistakes of excessive integration characteristic of US, European and Japanese firms.

4. THE CATALYTIC ROLE OF INWARD FDI

Inward FDI played an important catalytic role for knowledge creation during the critical early phase of the development of Taiwan's electronics industry. It exposed Taiwanese workers and managers to new organizational techniques, which, while not necessarily 'best practice', contributed to a gradual erosion of traditional, highly authoritarian and ultimately inefficient management practices. The need to comply with some minimum international quality standards gave rise to learning effects that spilled over to a wide spectrum of local enterprises due to the high turnover in Taiwan's skilled labour market.

Inward FDI also contributed to the development of local suppliers, at least for domestic market-oriented production. A combination of protection and local content requirements, directed especially at Japanese consumer electronics manufacturers, forced these companies to pull along their main Japanese component suppliers. Together they systematically groomed local vendors and established a broad range of local supplier networks.

FDI in Consumer Electronics

FDI-related linkages first emerged in consumer electronics. The pioneer was Philips which in 1961 established a large local manufacturing affiliate that produced TV sets, audio equipment, picture tubes and a variety of other related components. Originally this production facility was geared to the heavily protected local market, but by the mid-1960s domestic market-oriented production had been supplemented by export platform production. Philips Taiwan is now the exclusive production source for picture tubes for computer monitors within the entire Philips group, and it is among the three largest producers worldwide.[23] Similarly, Philips played a critical role in the successful launching of Taiwan Semiconductor Manufacturing Corporation (TSMC) which today is the world's leading silicon foundry.

In 1962 Matsushita followed suit with a large majority-owned joint venture in Keelung that produced both household appliances and consumer electronics, primarily TV sets.[24] Until the mid-1980s, when the group established a network of huge export platform affiliates in Malaysia and Thailand, this was one of Matsushita's main outposts in East Asia.[25] Matsushita's affiliate has been a *trend-setter* for Taiwan in factory automation (especially for printed circuit board assembly) and for the introduction of fastidious quality control management. In addition to being an incubator for local suppliers, Matsushita established Matsushita Electric Institute of Technology in 1981. With a work force of around 40 researchers, the institute's main functions are ASIC design and software engineering, especially the development of Chinese-language application programs.

Matsushita has also given rise to a broad range of knowledge spillovers to local companies, through both employment mobility and the formation of local start-up companies. One particularly interesting example is the case of Fulet Electronics Industrial Co. Ltd., a producer of high-end consumer electronics (author's interviews and Gold, 1986). The owner of this company is the son of C.C. Hong, Matsushita's original local joint venture partner. For many years C.C. Hong served as the chairman of Matsushita Electric (Taiwan). Yet, despite his 40 per cent share in the venture's capital, Japanese managers were clearly running the show. Hong was given a free hand to build up close technical and business ties with several hundred local suppliers. Building on his father's unbeatable connections within the local Taiwanese supplier community, Hong Junior (Hong Ming-t'ai) pursued a niche market strategy. By sourcing out a large part of manufacturing, Fulet can concentrate on design and product development. Two figures are revealing: Fulet claims to spend roughly 15 per cent of sales on R&D; and it classifies 15 per cent of its 800 employees as R&D personnel.[26] This example shows how a Taiwanese start-up company can exploit the domestic supplier networks that were originally established for Matsushita, in order to further its knowledge creation.

Matsushita's smaller rival Sanyo established its own production line in 1963, with a roughly similar product mix as Matsushita's, followed by Hitachi in 1965 and Sony in 1967. These Japanese firms also developed close links with local suppliers, but focused much longer on the domestic market; export platform production remained the exception.[27] Because the domestic market strategy could tolerate a certain degree of inefficiency and lower quality standards, Japanese consumer electronic affiliates in Taiwan had considerable decision autonomy not only for employment, work practices and salary, but also on how to organize production and procurement. A considerable number of local linkages were generated by these investments: local content was substantial, and gave rise to some domestic support industries, especially for low-end general purpose components.[28] All of these were powerful mechanisms for inter-organizational knowledge creation.

Toshiba pursued a different strategy.[29] During the 1950s it acquired a 5 per cent equity share in Tatung Co., Taiwan's only integrated electronics company. Originally Tatung served as an agent of Toshiba, selling its home appliances, consumer electronics and telecommunications equipment. In the 1960s, however, Toshiba granted a number of technology licences to Tatung, which became a supplier of key components, such as high-end compressors, CRT picture tubes and LCDs. This, in turn, led to other forms of co-operation. In the mid-1970s, for instance, Toshiba helped Tatung to capture OEM orders from Sears (the large US mass merchandiser), with the result that Tatung became one of the largest Taiwanese television exporters to the US. Tatung and Toshiba are now also engaged in a variety of OEM and technology co-operation agreements, involving monitors and other PC-related products.

During the 1970s Fujitsu followed with a similar approach: in 1973 it established a joint venture with Tatung to sell and service Fujitsu computer systems and peripherals. This subsequently led to a variety of manufacturing joint ventures and OEM contracts, including FDK Tatung (Thailand) Co. LTD/Bangpakong, an affiliate of Tatung's joint venture with Fujitsu, called Tatung Fujidenka Co. Taiwan. The mother company is in Yangmei, Taiwan and produces high-end soft ferrit cores for TV sets, video display terminals and a variety of electronic devices. FDK Tatung today is one of the market leaders for the capital and knowledge-intensive production of soft ferrit cores. The sales of this affiliate are mainly destined for affiliates of National (Matsushita), JVC, Murata and Tatung's Makolin affiliate in Thailand and Malaysia.[30]

FDI in Components

The first round of investment in consumer electronics and telecommunication equipment gave rise to a rapid growth in demand for electronic components. While most of the high value-added key components were imported, stringent local content requirements and increased local capacities resulted in the growth of local production. Starting from the mid-1960s Taiwan received substantial Japanese FDI in the production of electronic components.

The pioneer was Mitsumi Electric Corp., a medium-sized component producer. In 1967 its first affiliate was established in Kaohsiung, producing condensers, transformers (including coils), connectors, electro-mechanical subassemblies and other components. Two years later, in March 1969, this was followed by a second affiliate in Taipei, producing magnetic heads, small motors, plus a variety of subassemblies and other components. Similar investments were undertaken by TDK in 1968 (condensers, transformers and other components); by Hosiden in 1969, an Osaka-based producer of electromechanical components; by Mitsubishi Materials in June 1970 (condensers); and by Alps in 1970 (resistors, magnetic heads and other devices). In the 1970s most of the leading Japanese component producers set up shops in Taiwan or were engaged in consignment assembly with a growing share of output going to Japan or Japanese affiliates in Asia. In response to the combined effect of the yen appreciation and the domestic recession, Japanese electronics firms developed a regional supply base in the early 1990s that now includes higher-end components (Ernst, 1997b). These investments played an important catalytic role for knowledge creation in Taiwan's domestic supplier industry, through intense on-the-job training and employment turnover as well as through close linkages with local subcontractors.

Taiwan, however, has also now become a critical market for components and production equipment, especially for the computer industry and for the production of semiconductors, CRT picture tubes and displays. One consequence is that Japanese component manufacturers have extended the mix of products that they produce in Taiwan to include an increasing variety of computer-related components. This has helped to upgrade knowledge creation. For instance, both Sharp and Casio are today producing substantial volumes of mid-level STN-LCDs[31] in Taiwan. Similar developments have occurred in semiconductors: second-tier Japanese DRAM producers like Oki and Mitsubishi Electric Corp. (MELCO) have recently concluded important technology licensing, second-sourcing and joint development projects with some of the newly established Taiwanese DRAM producers. The same is now happening for large-size CRT picture tubes.

As Taiwanese component manufacturers have broadened their knowledge base, Japanese firms are willing to engage in joint ventures and co-development projects; this has led to substantial investments by Japanese production equipment vendors. For example, Japan's Shinetsu Handotai Co. has a 40 per cent share of Taiwan's market for silicon-wafer chips. The company's customers in Taiwan no longer wanted to depend on imports from Japan or from Shinetsu's affiliate in Malaysia, and insisted that Shinetsu establish a wafer fabrication plant in Taiwan. Given the huge demand from Taiwanese customers, Shinetsu complied and established a majority-owned $110 million joint venture in silicon-wafer fabrication. A second stage involving an additional $70 million investment is already planned. Shinetsu claims that, in terms of the technology used, 'there will be no difference between the factories in Taiwan and in Japan'.[32]

FDI in the Computer Industry

All investments reviewed so far have been in consumer electronics and component manufacturing. But what about FDI in the computer industry itself? In the early 1960s IBM established an affiliate in Taiwan where a few thousand people were employed wiring core frames by hand.[33] IBM's move to Asia did not occur in isolation: its competitors also established core plane wiring operations in Taiwan and Hong Kong (Harman, 1971). IBM thus gave rise to a new model of international production for American electronic firms: the redeployment of labour-intensive stages of final assembly to Asia. These investments, however, consisted of primitive 'screw-driver' assembly and thus generated very limited localized knowledge (Ernst, 1983).

The next round of computer-related FDI did not take place until the early 1980s. In 1982 DEC established a large integrated affiliate in Taiwan to produce a broad range of products: PC motherboards and chassis, monitors, terminals and printers. Today DEC Taiwan is the company's largest assembly line for desktop PCs and is also Taiwan's largest foreign-owned PC manufacturer. For Taiwan, DEC's investment had important positive effects on knowledge creation, through training as well as through the development of local suppliers. For instance, DEC Taiwan is a major OEM buyer of monitors from both Philips Taiwan and the Lite-on Group. DEC also sources a broad range of peripherals and components from local Taiwanese companies.

DEC's investment was followed two years later, in 1984, by Hewlett Packard (HP), which established a joint venture with Taiwan's Nanya Plastics (part of the Formosa plastics group) for producing multi-layered printed circuit boards. This venture involved a substantial transfer of technology and capabilities. On the basis of this successful project, HP has transferred more complex technology and thus has given a major boost to the development of Taiwan's capabilities in motherboard production. In co-operation with the Ministry of Economic Affairs and with large local conglomerates like the President Enterprises Group,[34] HP Taiwan has aggressively promoted the spread of computer-based factory automation.

Despite these and a few other cases of inward FDI in the computer industry, it is fair to say that such investments have played only a marginal role in the development of Taiwan's computer industry. Foreign computer companies did make an important contribution, yet such linkages worked primarily through the rapid proliferation of international outsourcing arrangements. These arrangements include subcontracting, consignment assembly and various forms of OEM contracts,[35] and are no longer confined to parts and components but involve high value-added support services such as product customization, product design and production technology.

5. KNOWLEDGE CREATION THROUGH GLOBAL PRODUCTION NETWORKS (GPNs)

American computer companies like Apple, IBM, DEC, Compaq and HP have been pioneers in the subcontracting of component manufacturing, contract assembly, the spread of OEM and more recently ODM (original design manufacturing) arrangements that enable them to concentrate on what they do best. Japanese computer companies only followed suit during the early 1990s, once their tight grip over their domestic market was challenged by the aggressive price war strategies of American computer companies.[36]

Spatial Dispersion

Today it is normal that the *supply chain* of a computer company spans different time zones and continents. For instance, final assembly is most likely dispersed to major growth markets in the US, Europe and Asia; microprocessors are sourced from the US; memory devices from Japan and Korea; motherboards from Taiwan; HDDs from Singapore; monitors from Korea, Taiwan and Japan; keyboards and power switch supplies from Taiwan, and so forth.

The picture gets blurred, however, as many of these suppliers in turn ship their products from widely dispersed overseas affiliates. Taiwanese OEM suppliers have shifted a growing share of their production to low-cost production sites in Southeast Asia and China. Since 1992 Taiwan's PC industry has experienced an extremely rapid expansion of overseas production. In value terms, the ratio of overseas production out of Taiwan's total PC production has increased from 10.4 per cent in 1992, to 14.9 per cent in 1993, 20.6 per cent in 1994, and 27.2 per cent in 1995.[37] In 1996 this ratio increased to almost 30 per cent. Throughout this short period annual growth in overseas production value was consistently over 70 per cent, which implies that overseas production today plays a critical role for the success and failure of Taiwan's PC industry.

Most of the overseas production of Taiwanese computer companies is concentrated in neighbouring regions in China (most of it in China's southern coastal provinces) and in Southeast Asia. For instance, out of the 95 overseas production sites of Taiwanese PC firms that have been registered by the Market Intelligence Centre (MIC) of Taiwan's Institute for Information Industry (III), 75 production sites (that is almost 80 per cent) have been located in East Asia (exclusive of Japan). China alone has attracted 41 investments, that is 43 per cent of the total.[38]

The logistic complexity of the new GPNs is not simply a result of their geographic spread; it is also a function of an *increasingly complex division of labour*. Each GPN combines different hierarchically structured and closely interacting sub-networks. For example, an American computer company such as IBM or Compaq is linked to first-tier contractors, say an American disk drive producer like Seagate with its GPN, or large Taiwanese OEM contractors like Acer. At the next level, we find medium-sized, specialized Taiwanese contractors like Delta Electronics, a major producer of switching power supplies that has production facilities in Thailand, China and Mexico. At the lowest levels, we find a myriad of sub-production networks, each centred around a small Taiwanese subcontractor, many of which have redeployed production to China or Southeast Asia. The complexity of such arrangements becomes clear when we look at the major customers list of a firm like Delta Electronics.[39] This list reads like a Who's Who in the computer industry and covers 24 leading computer companies from the US, Japan, Europe and Taiwan.[40]

In sum, Taiwanese firms in the electronics industry are deeply embedded in complex global production networks that involve transactions between a large number of different national production systems. The increasing complexity of GPNs, however, has also allowed small enterprises from a small nation to participate and upgrade their knowledge base.

Key Features of Global Production Networks

What factors have induced computer companies to increase their reliance on outsourcing and hence to establish GPNs? For a typical lead company in the PC business, the cost of components, software and services purchased from outside has increased from less than 60 per cent to more than 80 per cent of total (ex factory) production costs.[41] As external sourcing relations become geographically dispersed and increasingly complex, they are fraught with very high co-ordination costs: some firms report that the cost of co-ordinating such outside relations can exceed in-house manufacturing costs.[42] As a result, the focus of *cost reduction strategies* is *shifting from scale economies in manufacturing to a reduction of the cost of external sourcing* through rationalization and internationalization.

Outsourcing is also motivated by a *strategic* concern. In order to survive the extremely intense competition that is characteristic of the electronics industry, global competitors are forced to concentrate on product development (architectural design), while at the same time remaining a low-cost producer. In order to meet these goals firms tend to focus on R&D, the production of some key components, limited involvement in the final assembly of higher value-added products and marketing. By outsourcing most of the other activities, the lead company expects to reduce the high fixed capital costs and risks that result from large in-house production facilities. Finally, the lead company may exploit competition among potential suppliers to reduce production costs.

What are the interests of small suppliers from Taiwan? Participating in a GPN can provide various advantages, despite the continuing pressures for cost cutting (Ernst and Ravenhill, 1999; Ernst and O'Connor, 1989 and 1992; Ernst 1994b). Manufacturing on an OEM basis is a significant source of knowledge creation for affiliated firms. Not only do foreign purchasers supply specifications for OEM suppliers, they also frequently send their engineers to help local manufacturers to meet quality specifications. Knowledge is thus transmitted in OEM production, not only through the supply of blueprints, but also through the interaction of personnel and the transfer of more elusive, tacit dimensions of technology (Bell and Pavitt, 1993; Ernst and Lundvall, 1997/1998).

Once a supplier has acquired the relevant technology and technical expertise, it may be possible to use these in manufacturing components or final products on an OEM basis for other multinationals. Taiwanese firms often participate in more than one GPN. By manufacturing for a number of assemblers on an OEM basis, they can achieve economies of scale; longer production runs in turn justify the installation of capital equipment (and thus often better quality control) which otherwise would not be warranted. Furthermore, the provision of letters of credit by the foreign purchaser can enable the local manufacturer to borrow additional capital that can be invested in knowledge creation.

Another advantage for small suppliers is that participation in a production network avoids the expense of building distribution, sales and service networks. The costs of acquiring knowledge about foreign consumer preferences, and of setting up the distribution and service networks that are essential for penetrating foreign markets, pose a formidable challenge even to large multinationals. This is particularly true in Japan. Moreover, a move to own-brand production risks a disruption of the technological links with purchasers established under OEM relationships. Firms seeking to produce under their own brand name frequently find it more difficult to obtain technical advice from companies that increasingly perceive them as rivals. Manufacturers may gain a price premium from marketing under their own brand name, but this premium may be negative if consumers associate the brand with poor quality. Korean exporters of consumer electronic products appeared to suffer this fate in the Japanese market in the late 1980s, when inferior products coupled with inadequate service networks damaged the reputation of Korean manufacturers.

Marketing products under the firm's own brand name may place a company at the apex of the pyramid of technological and marketing capabilities, but Taiwanese companies have found that the costs incurred in setting up distribution, sales and service networks can outweigh the higher unit profits from OBM (original brand-name manufacturing). As they upgrade their production skills and capabilities, small suppliers are often able to change the bargaining relationship with the multinationals. There is evidence of Taiwanese firms moving from OEM to ODM, although still producing components or final products for sale under another company's brand name. In such circumstances, the balance of bargaining power between supplier and purchaser shifts, with the buyer becoming increasingly dependent on the skills of the local company. The ideal scenario from the perspective of the OEM supplier would be that the transfer of skills from the purchaser eventually leads to the hollowing out of the core competencies of the distributing company in the particular product line. This has been alleged to have occurred in the case of Samsung's manufacture of microwave ovens for GE (Magaziner and Patinkin, 1989).

Taiwan's Participation in Global Production Networks

Participation in international production networks has been of critical importance for the development of a highly flexible domestic supply base and its continuous upgrading. Manufacturing on an OEM basis has been the most important of such linkages. Taiwan's involvement in the OEM business has gone through different incarnations, from very simple arrangements to highly complex ones. Each of these has displayed a peculiar pattern of knowledge creation.

Taiwan's entry as a supplier for the international computer industry dates back to the mid-1960s. The breakthrough came in 1966 when IBM set up its International Procurement Office (IPO) and started to purchase computer parts and components from Taiwan. IBM's demanding procedures for product development, production ramp-up and quality control, as well as its gruelling requirements for vendor qualification, forced Taiwanese firms to radically upgrade their product quality. It also forced them to develop a broad spectrum of capabilities required for manufacturing as well as product design. *In the process of qualifying as an IBM supplier*, countless Taiwanese firms learned how to improve their input procurement and production control methods in order to cut costs, improve quality and to speed-up product development cycles and delivery. IBM engineers regularly visited Taiwanese suppliers, screened their production facilities and logistics and assisted them to improve their overall efficiency. These visits included countless missions by IBM engineers sent from the US or other affiliates of IBM's global production network.[43] Being an IBM supplier has been a great asset to many Taiwanese firms: buyers feel that they can trust a supplier who has been able to cope with the stringent IBM procurement requirements. Going through an IBM apprenticeship thus has helped Taiwanese firms to overcome their negative image of unreliability and shoddy quality and win more orders from other foreign computer companies. Nonetheless, Taiwan had to wait until the early 1980s before it was able to establish itself as a credible supplier. Two external developments served to change this situation.[44]

The first occurred in 1982 when the Taiwanese government responded to American pressure and declared the cloning of Apple II computers and video games illegal. With the benefit of hindsight it is obvious that this actually accelerated the move of Taiwanese firms to clone IBM PCs, which remained legal. These developments coincided with dramatic changes in the computer industry that created a window of opportunity for low-cost producers.[45] In contrast to mainframe and mini-computers, PC design is based on standard microprocessors and operating systems. As a result, computers became *mass-produced, standardized products (commodities)*. Barriers to entry to final assembly are low and the key to success for any 'cloning' strategy lies beyond manufacturing. A critical factor is *time-to-market*: the PC vendor needs guaranteed access to reasonably priced key components and the most up-to-date operating system; and its supply base for motherboards and other components must be able to respond fast and flexibly. Coping with the first prerequisite required close links with Intel and Microsoft, while the second prerequisite was perfectly matched to Taiwan's domestic supplier structure.

A second external factor facilitated Taiwan's entry into the international OEM business. In 1987 the US government imposed punitive tariffs of 100 per cent on Japanese PCs, both in response to US-Japanese trade conflicts in semiconductors and as a reaction to a perceived violation of COCOM rules by Toshiba.[46] The punitive tariff on Japanese suppliers allowed the Taiwanese to demonstrate to American computer companies that they could replace the Japanese suppliers with good products at good prices and that they could even deliver more quickly. Although the tariff was removed one year later, it was by then too late for Japanese computer companies to recover their lost share in the rapidly moving OEM market.

Taiwan's subsequent involvement in the OEM business has gone through different stages. Each of these stages displayed a peculiar pattern of knowledge creation. In order to understand these different knowledge effects, we need to open the black-box of OEM arrangements. An important finding that runs counter to established wisdom (for example, Hobday, 1995) is that successful upgrading does not necessarily require a shift from OEM to OBM. At the beginning OEM arrangements were very simple, both in terms of products and required capabilities. The focus was on low-end desktop PCs and labour-intensive peripherals, like computer mice and keyboards. The OEM customer provided detailed technical 'blueprints' and technical assistance to allow the Taiwanese contractor to produce according to specifications.

There is a broad consensus that Taiwanese firms were able to reap substantial benefits from this *easy* phase of OEM. Yet these simple forms of OEM also had substantial drawbacks. Suppliers became 'locked into' OEM relationships that hindered independent brand name recognition and marketing channels. Profit margins are thinner in OEM sales than in own brand sales, which in turn makes it difficult for suppliers to muster the capital needed to invest in R&D required for the development of new products. In response to these drawbacks, a number of Taiwanese computer companies tried to expand their share of own brand-name manufacturing (OBM) sales. In 1988, for example, the share of Taiwan brand-name to total PC sales stood at roughly 28 per cent; by 1989 it had risen to 40 per cent (*Eurotrade*, Taipei, Vol. 2, January 1990, p. 32). Yet the transition to OBM turned out to be difficult and only a handful of companies were able to succeed; most others failed and are now content to consolidate and upgrade their position as OEM suppliers. The result has been a drastic decline of OBM sales out of total Taiwanese computer sales. Most recent figures show that the share of OBM has declined from 34 per cent of all Taiwanese computer hardware sales in 1995 to less than 25 per cent in 1997. The story of this upgrading process can be seen through the lens of Taiwan's best-known computer company, Acer.

Acer's Peculiar Upgrading Experience

Acer's involvement in the PC cloning business dates back to 1983, when it was among the first Taiwanese companies to introduce an IBM XT/PC compatible. In the same year Acer had organized Taiwan's first International Distributor's Meeting, attended by delegates from over 20 countries. Building strong links with foreign distributors and OEM customers subsequently became an important priority, complementing Acer's strong domestic roots. The years following 1986 brought a number of early successes. At that time 32-bit microprocessors (MPU) were just beginning to appear on the market and Acer was able to beat IBM in announcing a 32-bit PC based on Intel's 386 MPU. During the same year Acer's subsidiary Continental Systems, Inc. (now Acer Peripherals) received two successive Excellence Rewards from ITT, acknowledging the high quality of its OEM products. After changing the company name to Acer in 1987,[47] the company got approval to list on the Taiwan stock exchange in 1988.

Acer's export success was not wholly dependent on OEM sales, however. These early triumphs led Acer's management to believe it could reduce this dependence and jump to producing its own brands. In 1988 Acer hired a senior IBM executive to reorganize the company with the explicit goal of transforming it into a global competitor. Expectations were running high. IBM was still considered the industry's role model; by copying key features of IBM, Acer expected to speed up its leapfrogging effort. In particular, the idea was to increase the company's vertical integration and generate a critical mass of proprietary assets that would enable Acer to develop its own brand name image.

This effort failed miserably. The IBM manager assumed that change could be imposed from above by forcing consensus on the local management. Such an aggressive top-down approach ran into stubborn opposition by Acer's managers and engineers who were used to a substantial amount of decision autonomy. Furthermore, Acer simply did not have the resources that are necessary to implement such a strategy. The peak of leapfrogging euphoria came in 1989, when Acer shipped its one millionth computer; was ranked for the first time by DATAMATION among the top 100 IT companies in the world; was chosen as one of the 'corporate stars of the future' by the *Wall Street Journal*; and was chosen by Texas Instruments (TI) as its joint venture partner for DRAM production in Taiwan. Insiders knew that TI's decision was based on the lavish financial package that Acer, in co-operation with the Taiwanese government, was able to offer.[48] For a broader public, however, the tie-up with TI conferred tremendous prestige.[49]

The shift in strategy was supposed to occur quickly. Acer projected that the share of OEM sales would decline from 40 per cent of total sales in 1988 to 25 per cent in 1992. Not only did Acer intend to compete through its own brand, but it also wanted to broaden its product portfolio. This led to a rapid succession of acquisitions which almost ended in disaster. Acer acquired Counterpoint Computers with the intention of using it to build a strong position in minicomputers, but the follow-up costs of technology development and marketing were way above Acer's expectations. Counterpoint lost $15 million in 1989 alone, almost as much as the $17 million that Acer had paid for it, and the firm was closed down. Undeterred, Acer tried again the following year, by acquiring Altos, an American producer of UNIX-based multi-user systems. At the time the expectation was that Altos's UNIX experience and distribution channels would help Acer to speed up its product diversification.[50] Bought for $94 million, the firm recorded a mere $125 million in sales in 1990, and was incurring heavy losses. Such losses continued for a few more years, but this time Acer also benefited. By acquiring Altos, the company was able to develop its computer networking capabilities and to enter the PC server market.

The awakening came in 1991 when Acer posted a loss ($23 million) for the first time. Acer's over-ambitious diversification strategy came at the worst possible moment. The PC industry worldwide was swept by a crippling price war, as a result of which almost all companies faced a serious profit squeeze. Taiwan's computer industry was particularly hard hit and went through a major shake-out. During the second half of 1991, 50 to 60 Taiwanese computer companies went out of business each month.[51] Most of these firms were small companies. One could argue that this was a healthy development, as it indicated a long overdue consolidation of this industry. Moreover, the disappearance of small firms from a sector under pressure seems to be a fairly normal occurrence in Taiwan; many of them reappear making something else or at a foreign location. Since 1991, however, a number of larger Taiwanese PC companies like Acer were in serious trouble too; some, such as Autocomputer, actually went out of business.

The spread of intense price wars constituted a major challenge for the Taiwanese computer industry, and readjustment came at a heavy cost. In order to sustain their position as OEM suppliers, Taiwanese firms had to implement drastic additional cost reductions at a time when Taiwan's traditional cost advantages were rapidly eroding. Fuelled by the appreciation of the NT$, the cost of land and labour in Taiwan exploded in the early

1990s, with the result that *Taiwan lost its comparative advantage as a low-cost production site*. At the same time Taiwan faced serious competitive threats both from *below* and from *above*. New low-cost competitors entered the fray in Southeast Asia and China, while South Korea strengthened its position as a supplier of scale-intensive components, like DRAMs, monitors, CRT picture tubes and display devices. Furthermore, Japanese firms, which lost market share both at home and in export markets, had now started to fight back and to develop much more aggressive global market penetration strategies.

Most Taiwanese firms made a conscious effort to consolidate their position in this field, but Acer pursued a rather different approach. While it consolidated its position as an OEM supplier, it simultaneously continued to pursue an aggressive OBM strategy. Rather than trying to reduce its reliance on OEM contracts, the objective now was to quickly increase the OEM share to 50 per cent. This part of the strategy has worked well. For desktop computers, Acer is one of the five Taiwan-based producers that have collectively come to dominate the OEM market: Tatung, Acer, DEC's Taiwan affiliate, FIC and AST's local affiliate. In addition to its strong position in desktop PCs, Acer has also become a major OEM supplier of notebook computers for Apple and Canon. The result was that, in 1994, the OEM share of Acer's PC sales had risen again to 35 per cent.

In sum, Acer's strategy is to leverage its OEM business to generate the necessary financial resources to pursue its OBM strategy and to further upgrade Acer's capabilities, especially in design and computer networking. The logical consequence is *a focus on mass production rather than on niche markets*. Acer's goal is to become one of the world's highest-volume producers of peripheral equipment, key components, sub-assemblies and design services, both for Acer's worldwide computer assembly plants and for leading international computer companies like Apple, Canon and Fujitsu. Acer describes its own competitive strength as 'the ability to market affordably-priced products quickly due to innovative production and distribution strategies, a component supply approach, a flexible and independent organization and economies of scale in manufacturing' (*The Acer Group Profile 1994*, p. 4).

Meanwhile, Acer's OBM strategy tries to combine the following, not always consistent goals: to establish a credible global brand image for a broad mix of 'affordably-priced products'; to improve its ability to market such products quickly and to adapt them in response to changing market requirements; to penetrate secondary markets in Asia, Latin America and elsewhere in order to gain economies of scale; and to use these countries as a test-ground for refining its globalization strategy. In these markets Acer aims to price its products 10 to 15 per cent below Compaq's prices. Gradually,

Acer would build its product and marketing capabilities in a few very limited *market niches*. Acer's acquisition of some American computer companies, like Altos, was one element of this approach, but much more important is the shift to digital consumer electronics and, possibly, Acer's pioneering role in the field of software design and distribution. These objectives serve the over-riding concern of developing an independent global brand image.

Until 1995 this dual strategy worked reasonably well: between 1993 and 1995, Acer's share price almost quintupled.[52] And in 1995 the group's consolidated sales revenues were $5.8 billion, up from $690 million in 1989. This quick and impressive turn-around owed a great deal to sheer luck and to industry-specific factors that were beyond Acer's control. Probably of greatest importance was the strong demand for DRAM chips which pushed up profit margins for this product. Without the windfall profits of TI-Acer's DRAM joint venture, Acer would probably still have been suffering from its over-ambitious diversification strategy. In 1993, 90 per cent of Acer's net earnings were generated by TI-Acer, and its share in Acer's 1995 net earnings was still as high as 45 per cent. This, however, has drastically changed since 1996. As a result of the free fall of DRAM prices, TI-Acer has ceased to act as a cash cow for Acer's OBM strategy.[53]

As for Acer's core PC business, profit margins have improved. The surprise success of Acer's multimedia home personal computer in 1994 has helped to improve the company's position.[54] In 1995 Acer became one of the top ten PC suppliers to the US market. Since then, however, not much has moved. In 1995 the US market still accounted for roughly 26 per cent of Acer's worldwide sales, and in 1996 Acer America went into the red again. While Acer retained its top position in a number of rapidly growing, yet still quite secondary markets like Indonesia, Malaysia, Mexico and South Africa, the overall growth of sales revenues for computers has slowed down and Acer has still not succeeded in expanding its OBM market share in Japan and China.

All of this does not imply that Acer's strategy has failed altogether. Rarely has a company grown so fast, and rarely has a small firm from a small nation been able to build up such a broad range of capabilities and to introduce far-reaching organizational innovations during a relatively short period of time. Yet it also shows that there is no easy and quick short-cut to success and that leapfrogging is an illusionary concept that should be discarded.[55] Developing a firm's knowledge base is a time-consuming and laborious process: at each stage of its growth, new barriers arise that require a period of consolidation. The more Acer progresses and grows, the more demanding will be the barriers with which it has to cope. This precludes a frontal attack on the market leaders. Attacking from the sidelines is the only realistic option. This is certainly true as long as Acer has not yet reached a size that qualifies it for Fortune 500 membership. The key to Acer's success is that it has pursued a gradual market penetration strategy: it avoids direct confrontation and pursues markets where the market leaders are not present.[56] Acer's OBM strategy thus remains primarily focused on non-OECD markets, while at the same time it continues to upgrade its capabilities as an OEM supplier. This shows that Chandler is right in emphasizing the difficulties to overcome the *first mover* advantages of large multinationals (Chandler, 1990). Yet Acer's story also shows that a small firm from a small nation can enter and grow in the rapidly moving computer industry, provided that it pursues a realistic market penetration strategy.

The Dynamics of Knowledge Creation in OEM Arrangements

Developing a global brand image is costly and involves extreme risks. Acer's approach to 'attack from the sidelines' and to focus its OBM strategy on non-OECD markets is one realistic response to this dilemma. As for market penetration in the US, Japan and Europe, Taiwanese computer firms will have to rely however for quite some time on OEM contracts. This is why upgrading Taiwan's OEM position is currently the appropriate strategic priority. Let us look at some examples.

Since 1993 Taiwan became the main OEM supplier of PC-related products for leading American and European computer manufacturers and distributors. Compaq for instance now sources its monitors from ADI, Philips Taiwan and TECO; notebooks from Inventa, power supplies from Lite-on and Delta, and mouse devices from Logitech Taiwan and Primax. Probably the most interesting arrangement is that with Inventa, a company that has earned a reputation for innovative notebook design and that has already supplied notebooks on an ODM basis to Dell and Zenith, now an affiliate of the French computer firm Bull. Inventa is part of the family-owned Inventec business group that is involved in a wide range of products and services, but is most well-known for calculators and telephones.

Logitech Taiwan provides another illustration of how complex global production networks have become in the computer industry; it also highlights the high volatility of the OEM business and the need to continuously upgrade product mix and capabilities (Jolly and Bechler, 1992 and author's interviews). Founded in 1981 in Switzerland and incorporated a few months later in the US, Logitech is the world's largest producer of computer tracking devices (mice and trackballs). In 1987 Logitech shifted production to Taiwan and established a large volume production line in Hsinchu Science Park. Taiwan's main attraction was that it offered a well-developed supply base for parts, qualified people and a rapidly expanding PC industry. In 1995, however, Logitech shifted all of its production from Taiwan to China. The result has been a drastic decline of Taiwan's share of the global mouse market from almost 75 per cent in 1994 to 65 per cent in 1996. At the same time Logitech continues to use the same Taiwanese suppliers that have now set up shop close to Logitech's new location in China.

Compaq provides another example of the increasing complexity of Taiwan's OEM arrangements. In a recent *turnkey production* contract with Mitac, Compaq has outsourced all stages of the value chain for some of its desktop PCs, except marketing for which it retains sole responsibility. Other foreign computer companies have followed Compaq's example. For instance, IBM signed an agreement with the Acer Group where Acer would use its global production network in developing countries to assemble lower-end IBM desktop and laptop PCs and to distribute and service them. Turnkey production arrangements constitute an important innovation and show how rapidly OEM relationships have moved beyond production to encompass an increasing variety of knowledge-intensive, high-end support services. The spread of such broad cross-value chain arrangements shows that leading foreign computer companies are confident that Taiwan's computer industry is now sufficiently well integrated to serve as a one-stop shopping centre.

Japanese PC manufacturers have also drastically increased their OEM contracts with Taiwanese firms for desktop PCs, motherboards, terminals and monitors, and a variety of other PC-related products. NEC for instance gets monitors and motherboards from Tatung and Elite, Fujitsu has relied primarily on OEM supplies from Acer, and Epson, Canon, Hitachi, Sharp and Mitsubishi have all become major OEM customers.

Upgrading Is Possible Within the OEM Trajectory

It is important to emphasize that these developments benefit rather than harm Taiwan's computer industry. This reflects important changes in the competitive dynamics of the computer industry. Paradoxically, an increasing concentration of the global computer industry has been accompanied by a growing reliance on global outsourcing: the top five industry leaders, which are all Taiwan's OEM clients, have increased their global market share from roughly 20 per cent during the early 1990s to almost 50 per cent. Their main strength is the definition of architectural standards and their global brand image. These global market leaders are at the cutting-edge of product development, but they outsource almost everything else. Close interaction with these industry leaders provides Taiwanese firms with *a constant flow of precious feedback information* on product design, new architectural standards, leading-edge production technology and sophisticated quality control and logistics procedures. Close links with these industry leaders act as a powerful vehicle for a further strengthening of the learning and innovation capabilities of Taiwanese computer firms.

We have seen that OEM contracts have now become much more demanding: they require a broad range of sophisticated capabilities that cover most if not all stages of the value chain. Taiwanese firms now need to provide more sophisticated services, including design and global supply chain management.[57] While in 1993 roughly one half of all PCs supplied by Taiwanese OEM suppliers were based on Taiwanese designs, this share today has increased to more than 70 per cent.[58] Of even greater importance is a tendency to extend OEM contracts to comprise an integrated package of higher-end support services, as illustrated in the turnkey production contracts of Compaq with Mitac, and of IBM with Acer. This implies that, with the exception of hard-core R&D and strategic marketing, Taiwan's OEM supplier community must be able to shoulder all steps in the production chain and the co-ordination functions necessary for global supply chain management.

A major prerequisite for Taiwanese firms is a capacity to assist foreign OEM customers in the management of their global supply chain. All the leading computer companies have drastically rationalized their global supply chain and are moving rapidly toward order-based production. In their choice of OEM suppliers, they demand a capacity for just-in-time delivery: for Taiwanese suppliers, this implies that speed and flexibility of response are critical; Taiwanese suppliers also must establish their own global network of plants and sales affiliates in close proximity to major computer markets. In other words, organizational innovation is of increasing importance and can go a long way in compensating for weaknesses in technological innovation.

These fundamental changes in OEM relationships are producing a new division of labour between large Taiwanese computer majors and SMEs. *Large firms appear to rely more on OEM contracts*, while *SMEs are much more active in ODM*. For instance, OEM orders for desktop computers are all concentrated on a select group of large companies, such as Tatung, Acer, DEC Taiwan, FIC and MITAC. The same is true for other scale-sensitive products such as monitors and modems. This sounds counter-intuitive, but *OEM contracts come in large orders*; they typically generate razor-thin profit margins. Economies of scale and scope are of critical importance, and large firms are better placed to reap such economies. Time and again, we thus find that Chandler's insistence on the continuous importance of scale and scope economies makes perfect sense, even in a fast moving sector like the computer industry (Chandler, 1990). Moreover, only a large firm can avoid becoming overly dependent on one particular customer.

Smaller firms may find it too risky to depend on large OEM contracts, as each of these contracts normally surpasses their maximum production capacity. They prefer to shift to ODM contracts where they have greater chances to sustain a diversified customer base and charge higher prices. In other words, *SMEs are under greater pressure* relative to large Taiwanese firms to improve their design capabilities to become credible niche market players within the overall OEM market. Many of these SMEs will not succeed, but those that do have good chances to grow and to improve their competitive position.

6. CONCLUSIONS

This chapter has been based upon an alternative conceptual framework that centres on the *co-evolution of domestic and international knowledge linkages*. This framework allowed us to analyse what permits small firms to compete in globalized high-tech industries. The chapter demonstrates that *inter-organizational knowledge creation* is critical for small firms that compete in the computer industry. If well organized and managed, such external knowledge linkages can effectively compensate for some of the original size-related disadvantages of small firms, at least for a certain period of time. However it is also shown that *external linkages are no substitute for intra-organizational knowledge creation*. This confirms Edith Penrose's observation that 'a firm's rate of growth is limited by the growth of knowledge within it' (Penrose, 1959/1995, Foreword to the 3rd edn, pp. XVI and XVII).

It has also to be emphasized that inter-organizational knowledge creation is *not confined to regional clusters* or to the nation state. In industrialized countries, many of these external knowledge linkages are with *domestic* organizations. This is very different for a small developing country. When Taiwan began to enter the computer industry during the late 1970s, domestic linkages did not exist or were at best embryonic. International linkages thus were initially of primary importance. This is in line with the findings of research on technological learning in developing countries.[59] Two types of international linkages have been distinguished: inward FDI and the participation of Taiwanese firms in global production networks established by foreign electronics companies.

Inward FDI has played an important catalytic role for knowledge creation during the early phase of the development of Taiwan's electronics industry. Participation in global production networks has been of critical importance for the development of a highly flexible domestic supply base and its consequent rapid internationalization. Manufacturing on an OEM basis has been the most important of such linkages. Taiwan's involvement in the OEM business has gone through different stages. Each of these stages displayed a peculiar pattern of knowledge creation. It started with very simple OEM arrangements that covered low-end desktop PCs and labour-intensive peripherals. The OEM customer provided detailed technical 'blueprints', components and technical assistance to allow the Taiwanese contractor to produce according to specifications.

Most of the literature has focused on this easy phase of OEM: there is a broad consensus that, during this phase, Taiwanese firms were able to reap substantial benefits. In response to their drawbacks, a number of Taiwanese computer companies have tried, during the early 1990s, to expand their share of own brand-name manufacturing sales. Most of them failed and are now content to consolidate and upgrade their position as OEM suppliers. This is hardly surprising: developing a global brand image is costly and involves extreme risks; it is way beyond the reach of most Taiwanese companies, with the possible exception of some larger companies like Acer. It is shown that, paradoxically, this increasing reliance on OEM arrangements has had positive effects for knowledge creation in Taiwan's computer industry. Contrary to established wisdom, successful upgrading does not necessarily require a shift from OEM to OBM.

All this implies that requirements for knowledge creation have become much more demanding: Taiwan's OEM supplier community must now be able to master all steps in the production chain, with the exception of hard-core R&D and strategic marketing. In addition, Taiwanese OEM suppliers must be able to perform for their customers co-ordination functions that are necessary for global supply chain management.

Moreover, benefits from international linkages do not come automatically. Of critical importance are *government policies* that have created a set of innovative institutions and incentives conducive for inter-organizational knowledge creation (see also Chapter 4 in this volume). Of equal importance are a variety of *domestic linkages* that range from informal peer group networks to a variety of innovations in firm organization that attempt to combine the scale advantages of large firms with the speed and flexibility of smaller firms. Contrary to conventional wisdom, *large firms* have played a central role in the co-ordination and development of the Taiwanese computer industry; they have also acted as *important sources for knowledge creation in SMEs*.

NOTES

1.   If not indicated otherwise, data on Taiwan's computer industry are courtesy of the Market Intelligence Centre of the Institute for Information Industry (III), Taipei.
2.   'PC network products' are defined as 'products that are used for LANs (Local Area Networks), PSTN (Public Switched Telephone Network), ISDN (Integrated Services Digital Network), ASDL (Asymmetric Digital Subscriber Loop) and cable modems'. Main

products include 'network interface cards, hubs, bridging switches, modems and routers'. Definitions are taken from: *Electronic Computer Glossary*. Add-on cards include sound, video and graphics cards. Of these, video cards display higher than average profit margins.

3.   There is a rich body of research, based on the assumptions of evolutionary economics, that specifies what type of capabilities are required and how the development of such capabilities affects firm organization. In addition to the references in note 1, see Lundvall (1988 and 1992); Carlsson and Stankiewicz (1991); Teece, Pisano and Shuen (1997); Christensen (1996); Foray and Lundvall (1996); Foss (1996); Llerena and Zuscovitch (1996); and Malerba and Orsenigo (1996a). For an application of this theoretical approach to research on developing countries, see Ernst, Mytelka and Ganiatsos (1998), and Ernst and Lundvall (1998). Much of the literature on firm capabilities, however, focuses on large multidivisional corporations and fails to discuss how small enterprises can develop such capabilities. Exceptions are Acs and Audretsch (1992); and Maskell (1996a and 1996b).

4.   For the underlying argument, see Acs and Audretsch (1992). For a critical assessment, see Harrison (1994).

5.   For details, see Shieh (1990) and Lam and Lee (1992, p. 112). Individual firms often bid for contracts beyond their own capacities; once a supplier gets the contract, it calls on other firms, often competitors, to help fill the order.

6.   For an analysis of Silicon Valley-type production networks, see Saxenian (1990).

7.   Chandler (1990), remains the most authoritative source. Economies of scale and scope in the computer industry are analysed in Flamm (1988 and 1990); Ferguson (1990); Ernst and O'Connor (1992); and Ernst (1997c).

8.   'While standardization appears to be a necessary consequence of the attempts of economic agents to exploit economies of scale and to avoid dealing with impossible amounts of information, this may also lead to difficulties for innovative activities' (Andersen, 1996, p.98).

9.   The primary source for such 'user-producer linkages' remains Lundvall (1988).

10.   The Statute for Investment by Foreign Nationals was first promulgated in July 1954 to attract foreign companies. In November 1955, this was followed by the Statute for Investment by Overseas Chines whose purpose was to tap into the experiences and capital of the Overseas Chinese communities in Hong Kong and Southeast Asia. Finally, the Statute for the Encouragement of Investment was enacted in September 1960 (San Gee and Kuo, 1998).

11.   For an analysis of such crowding-out effects on potential domestic investment in Southeast Asia, see Lim and Fong (1991).

12.   San Gee (1995a, table 4). The real interest rates for secured loans in Taiwan were 14.14 per cent, 9.0 per cent, 8.05 per cent and 9.7 per cent respectively in 1965, 1970, 1975 and 1985. There was only one exception: in 1980, the rate fell to -2.80, which was primarily due to the second oil crisis in that year. Note that these figures are adjusted for inflationary effects.

13.   Scitovsky (1990, Figure 4.1) shows that, in most years between 1971 and 1980, Korea's corporate sector debt to equity was between 310 and 380, while Taiwan's ratio was much lower between 160 and 180. This is consistent with more recent figures quoted in Fields (1995, table 4-5) which show that in 1985, the debt-equity ratio of Korean manufacturing firms was nearly 350, relative to a ratio of 120 for Taiwan. See also the figures quoted in Patrick and Park (1994).

14.   ING Barings estimate, quoted in *The Economist*, November 7, 1998, p. 13.

15.   For the most recent relevant developments of Taiwan's industrial policy, with particular reference to electronics, see Kuo and Wang, Chapter 4 in this volume; for its evolution over time see San Gee and Kuo (1998); San Gee (1995a); Kobayashi (1995); Meaney (1994); Kajiwara (1993); Liu (1993); Schive (1990 and 1993); and Wong Poh Kam (1995).

16.   Externality requirements vary, depending on the market segment and the stage of development of a particular industry. For consumer electronics, they are obviously less demanding than for semiconductors. And within the same product group, i.e. semiconductors, such requirements become much more complex, once the focus shifts

from low-end discrete devices for consumer applications to higher-end design-intensive devices.

17. Similar stories abound for foreign companies as well: RCA, the incubator of Taiwan's semiconductor industry, Philips, IBM Taiwan, AT&T Taiwan, Matsushita, Toshiba, Sanyo, and Fujitsu.

18. See Liu, Liu and Wu (1994). The spread of such business groups partly reflects the impact of government policies; starting in the late 1950s, the government shifted its emphasis away from public enterprises to the private sector, providing guidance and essential externalities. This has set the stage for the growth of private firms.

19. Questionnaire survey, conducted in July 1992 for the Ministry of Economic Affairs, covering a sample of 4,137 private manufacturing companies in Taiwan. See Liu, Liu and Wu (1994, p. 51).

20. A similar system apparently works for leading-edge components: while price levels, of course, are substantially higher than for the more vintage-type components, they still tend to be below price levels on the spot market.

21. Based on author's interviews at Acer. Similar approaches have been developed by other leading Taiwanese computer manufacturers like Mitac and FIC.

22. Acer hired an IBM executive to assist its reorganization in 1988, with little success; however, the crisis of 1991 spurred a new round of organizational innovation (*Business Week*, November 27, 1995, p. 73).

23. Philips Taiwan's integrated monitor facilities were singled out by Cor Boonstra, Philips' president, as one of the core activities of the group, as it 'supplies leading brands' (quoted from: 'Philips strategy on electrical goods a year away', *Financial Times*, February 14, 1997).

24. NEC actually was the first Japanese electronics company to set up a production affiliate in Taiwan: in March of 1958 it established a small plant assembling communication equipment for the local market.

25. Until March 1989, Matsushita had invested roughly $500 million in its Taiwan affiliate which then employed 5 300 local workers and recorded sales of Yen 73.7 billion (*The Japan Economic Journal*, July 1, 1989, p. 4).

26. While these figures may be somewhat exaggerated, industry insiders confirm that Fulet does concentrate on higher-end support services relative to manufacturing. The company adds value through sophisticated design features and thus is able to charge premium prices.

27. This is in line with a general tendency of Japanese electronics firms to postpone the shift from exports to offshore export platform production until the catalytic effect of the yen appreciation in 1985 finally forced them to establish export platform production lines in Southeast Asia. See Ernst (1997b).

28. This, however, came at the expense of cost efficiency and quality which, due to the heavy protection provided to the domestic market, were only of secondary concern.

29. This arguably results from the fact that Toshiba resembles the Siemens and Hitachi model in its relatively broad-based product mix that covers heavy electrical equipment and industrial electronics as well as consumer electronics.

30. Tatung's Makolin affiliate in Malaysia is an interesting case which indicates what unusual forms of international co-operation are possible today. It is a joint venture between Tatung's affiliate Chunghwa Picture Tubes and the Korean Dugo Electronics Company. Its main products are deflection yokes for 14, 20 and 21-inch colour tubes. Again, this affiliate supplies Tatung's affiliates in the region as well as affiliates of Japanese TV set makers.

31. The super-twist-nematic liquid crystal display (STN-LCD) has lower contrast, a worse viewing angle, and a slower response time than the more advanced thin-film-transistor (TFT) LCD, but is less expensive to produce.

32. Interview with Richard Kuo, president of Topco Scientific, the Taiwan agent for Shinetsu, in *FEER*, 10/12/95, p. 66.

33. Pugh (1984, pp. 250-51): 'It was slow, tedious, meticulous work, stringing wires in just the right manner through each of the thousands of tiny cores in each core plane. But the cost of labor there was so low that it was actually a few dollars [per unit] cheaper than with full

automation in Kingston (New York state)'.

34. President Enterprises is a huge conglomerate that started out in the retail sector and with food processing and that now has established a major presence in China and South East Asia. In 1995 the group acquired the Taiwan operations of the once powerful US Wang computer company. Through its Wang affiliate, President Enterprises has established a joint venture with HP with the purpose of developing Taiwan's market for factory automation and information networks (*Computergram*, April 20, 1994).

35. Definitions of what constitutes an *OEM* (original equipment manufacturing) contract keep changing. Probably the most widely accepted definition refers to arrangements between a brand name company (the customer) and the contractor (the supplier) where the *customer provides detailed technical blueprints and most of the components to allow the contractor to produce according to specifications*. Using this definition of OEM arrangements, we can then distinguish *ODM* (original design manufacturing) as arrangements where the *contractor is responsible for design and most of the component procurement, with the brand name company retaining exclusive control over marketing*.

36. Until the mid-1980s, Japanese computer firms were actually major OEM suppliers to American computer companies. We will see in a moment what factors have enabled Taiwanese firms to bypass Japanese companies as leading OEM suppliers.

37. In 1995 keyboards had the highest overseas production ratio (OPR), with 86 per cent of Taiwan's total production value being produced overseas. Other products with high OPRs are: power switching supply (77 per cent), monitors (almost 50 per cent), motherboards (37 per cent), and mouse devices (24 per cent).

38. Questionnaire survey by MIC/III, conducted in 1996.

39. Interview at Delta Electronics, June 7, 1995.

40. Acer, Alcatel, AST, Apple, Canon, Compaq, DEC, Epson, Hewlett Packard, Hitachi, IBM, Intel, Microtek, Matsushita, Mitsubishi, Motorola, NCR, NEC, Philips, Rockwell, Synoptics, Tatung, Thomson, and Toshiba.

41. These and the following figures are based on company interviews, as reported in Ernst and O'Connor (1992, pp. 34 and 37).

42. Such costs are typically defined as 'all incremental costs associated with dealing with suppliers remote from the initial design site and/or the final assembly site', with communication costs and administrative overheads absorbing the largest share (Ernst and O'Connor, 1992, ibid.).

43. According to one source at IBM Taiwan, the mother company dispatched over 400 such missions during the 1980s in order to assist Taiwanese suppliers (author's interview at IBM Taiwan).

44. Callon (1994); Wong Poh Kam (1995) and author's interviews in the Taiwanese computer industry since 1987.

45. Flamm (1988); Ernst and O'Connor (1992, chapters II and IV); Langlois (1992) and Ernst (1997c).

46. Toshiba's clandestine sale of a complex numerically controlled machine tool to the Soviet Union, judged to be of high value for arms production, provoked the action.

47. Acer is Latin for 'sharp, acute, able and facile'.

48. Texas Instruments' strategy is to choose wafer fabrication locations where most of the investment costs are shouldered by local governments. See Ernst (1994b).

49. By 1989, Acer's consolidated sales revenues were less than $690 million and it had around 5,500 employees.

50. *Business Times* (Singapore), 2/11/1992.

51. China Economic News Service, 12/4/1991.

52. 'Acer's Edge: PCs to Go', *Fortune*, 10/30/95.

53. In response to the accelerating fall of DRAM prices, Texas Instruments, in 1998, withdrew from this joint venture, and from the DRAM business altogether.

54. Its US affiliate was among the first firms to anticipate the demand for home multimedia computers – high-end systems with CD-ROM drives that play compact disc-based software with sharp graphics and stereo sound. Much of this was good luck. Acer just happened to

have the right product at the right time ready for the right market (Zielinger, M. 'Ace in the Hole. Taiwan's Acer makes surprising comeback in America', *Far Eastern Economic Review*, 1/26/95, p. 52).

55. For an early critique, see Ernst and O'Connor (1989, chapter II).
56. Kotler *et al.* (1985) remains the classic source.
57. For the concept of *global supply chain management*, see Lee and Billington (1995) and Levy (1995).
58. Design, in this context, includes the capacity to make quick changes in the configuration of motherboards in order to be able to integrate the latest microprocessor generation. While this is a very demanding requirement, it is quite different from the capacity to define architectural standards and create new markets.
59. This research has clearly established that successful late industrialization critically depends on the international sourcing of knowledge. Examples include Dahlman, Ross-Larson and Westphal (1987); Bell and Pavitt (1993); Nelson and Pack (1995); Kim (1997); Lall (1997); Ernst and Lundvall (1997/1998); and Ernst, Ganiatsos and Mytelka (1998).

6. New Challenges for Industrial Clusters and Districts: Global Production Networks and Knowledge Diffusion

Dieter Ernst, Paolo Guerrieri, Simona Iammarino and Carlo Pietrobelli

1. THE VARIETY OF INDUSTRIAL CLUSTERS AND DISTRICTS AND THEIR EVOLUTION OVER TIME

The main findings reported in this book suggest three inter-related propositions. First, there is no one best model for organizing an industrial district or an industrial cluster, since a diversity of institutional arrangements is possible and each has proved successful in different circumstances. Second, clusters are not cast in iron, but they evolve over time. The third proposition is that globalization reshapes the upgrading options for SME-based clusters, by providing a variety of international knowledge linkages. In a nutshell, we argue that globalization changes both the concept of proximity and the scope of competition: a necessary prerequisite for competitive survival is the capacity to foster the co-evolution of local and global linkages and networks, to develop new interactive modes of knowledge creation and to adjust strategy and organization at short notice.

The first two propositions are fully confirmed by the reorganization of both the Italian industrial districts and Taiwanese SME-based clusters, particularly over the past decade, as assessed in this volume. The typical uniformity in the growth process of SME systems, experienced during the 1970s and 1980s in Italy's local systems, has come to an end. New diversified patterns of growth have been observed and the range of options chosen expands when attempting to draw international comparisons. The empirical analysis, based on a survey carried out in some Italian IDs specialized in textiles and clothing, shows that the reaction to the globalization challenge may differ greatly even among IDs specialized in the same industrial sector. No common and unidirectional development pattern has proved valid any more, and different avenues have been followed to face the new competitive challenges posed by the globalization of markets and technology. Moreover, the scope and variety of inter-firm organization is continuously expanding, in relation to the increasing internationalization of economic and innovative activities.

Among the crucial factors explaining the evolution of the IDs' industrial organization are the (external) inducements derived from technology and technological change that appear important in a world increasingly shaped by the new ICT regime and the growing role of the knowledge economy.

The recent approaches to the analysis of spatial agglomeration of economic activities have gradually shifted the attention from traditional purely economic factors to the mechanisms of knowledge diffusion and accumulation established in spatial clusters of related industries; where learning dynamics and knowledge exchanges are embedded in a distinct environment of interactions among different subjects, sharing common attitudes towards particular types of learning. Dynamic agglomeration economies are likely to affect growth rates and have been considered as central to assess the patterns of development of industrial districts and their reaction to the rapid change brought about by the global competition.

The changes in the technology paradigms and trajectories that crucially affect the foundations of competitiveness are increasingly shaped by the internationalization process and contribute to determine the form of company strategy, especially for what concerns inter-firm attitudes, and the industrial organization prevailing within an enterprise cluster. The shift in the technological paradigm that applies to all sectors requires a substantial industrial reorganization. Again, firms traditionally operating within IDs need to learn to source their technological knowledge from the most convenient locations outside the district, and to reorganize their knowledge linkages from a cluster-based approach to a global and broader approach, such as that represented by the global production network model.

Our focus in this concluding chapter is in particular on the third proposition, that is, the spatial impact of globalization, especially on knowledge diffusion and innovation. In the light of the findings of our book, an important objective is to assess and clarify some propositions on the spatial impact of globalization that have been proposed by innovation and growth theorists (for example, Antonelli, 1999), trade economists (for example, Krugman, 1995), economic geographers (for example, Swann *et al.*, 1998; Scott, 1998), and sociologists (for example, Castells, 1998) that are giving rise to intense policy debates.

2. THE SPATIAL IMPACT OF GLOBALIZATION: RECONSIDERING THE AGGLOMERATION ECONOMIES ARGUMENT

The question of how globalization affects the geographical dispersion of knowledge and innovation, and whether this fosters or constrains local capability formation, has enjoyed an important role in theoretical debates on the role of FDI and multinational corporations (for example, Dunning, 1998). More recently this question has also received attention in innovation theory, the theory of the firm and economic geography (Chandler *et al.*, 1998).

The dominant position has been that innovation, in contrast to most other stages of the value chain, is highly immobile: it remains tied to specific locations, despite a rapid geographical dispersion of markets, finance and production (Archibugi and Michie, 1997). The main reason for such spatial stickiness is the interactive nature of innovation (Kline and Rosenberg 1986; Lundvall, 1988): it requires dense knowledge exchanges between users and producers, much of it being tacit knowledge. Such information-rich transfers require localized clusters within a nation, or even better, an industrial district or micro-region (Porter, 1990; Lundvall, 1992; Saxenian, 1994; Storper and Salais, 1997; Markusen, 1998). This reflects the importance of dynamic agglomeration economies: co-location facilitates a continuous, intense and rapid exchange of new ideas about technical, organizational and production improvements.

Thus knowledge and innovation do not easily migrate across borders: they do not automatically follow, once production moves. If this is true, this would imply that even while globalization extends its reach beyond trade and finance, giving rise to an extensive relocation of production, this may not help to reduce the huge international gaps in knowledge and innovation. For industrial countries, the spatial stickiness of innovation may foster attempts to sustain their technological superiority. For developing countries, however, spatial stickiness of innovation may fundamentally constrain their sources of growth, and hence perpetuate global inequality.

Proximity exerts a powerful constraining effect on the location of economic activities: industries tend to agglomerate and cluster in particular geographical locations, giving rise to persistent patterns of national and regional specialization. Alfred Marshall's pioneering concept of *externalities* (1890/1916, p. 271) helps identify both static and dynamic economies of agglomeration. While static agglomeration economies focus on efficiency gains resulting from scale economies, transaction and transport costs and input-output linkages, dynamic agglomeration economies highlight the central role of learning and knowledge creation.

Marshall's important observations have been forgotten for a long time:

until recently neo-classical economists have neglected the agglomeration or clustering of related activities. Since Krugman (1991a, 1995), economic geography has been re-established as a respectable topic for mainstream economists. This has brought back into economic theory increasing returns and other anomalies like the path dependency of spatial location. Unfortunately these debates have remained trapped in the static efficiency paradigm, missing the importance of knowledge creation and learning.[1]

Now, however, there is a growing literature that analyses the dynamics of spatial agglomeration. It is argued that clustering effects are particularly important for knowledge externalities and spillovers (Porter, 1990; Enright, 1998; Spender, 1998; Porter and Sølvell, 1998; OECD, 1999). Concentrations of companies succeed when they co-operate as well as compete; the focus of co-operation is on the sharing of knowledge, skills and technologies among companies and with public agencies.

Dynamic agglomeration economies are considered to be an important determinant of firm behaviour. Resources and capabilities that are critical for a firm's competitive success 'can often be found inside a region, rather than within any single firm'; 'regional clusters often involve activities that are shared across firms within the cluster' (Enright, 1998, pp. 315-16). A regional cluster provides access to specific resources and capabilities that are difficult to reproduce otherwise; it enables a firm to engage in peculiar types of co-ordination and organization; and it allows the firm to share activities with other cluster participants (Enright, 1998, pp. 328-36).

Attempts to construct a neo-Marshallian agglomeration theory are a positive development, as long as we remain conscious of some inherent limitations. It is not possible to apply this concept today without substantial changes.[2] We argue that globalization has created an explosive mix of forces that facilitate international knowledge diffusion, increasing the variety of international knowledge linkages. This creates new opportunities and challenges for the development and upgrading of SME-based industrial districts.

We need, therefore, an explicit analysis of the impact of globalization on agglomeration economies and on international knowledge diffusion. In this book some new insights and empirical evidence have been put forward along these lines. In addition, research on globalization has clearly established that the centre of gravity has shifted beyond the national economy. Cross-border linkages proliferate, with the result that no country can exist any longer in isolation. The same is true for regions and industrial clusters. They are rapidly becoming internationalized, and increasingly depend on international linkages (Dunning, 1998) to import key inputs and to export outputs. Such external linkages cover both tangibles like materials and machinery, and intangibles like finance and knowledge. A significant increase in the share of the latter is an important distinguishing feature of current rounds of globalization.

3. CONCENTRATED DISPERSION

Despite the fundamental advantages of keeping production at home and at close proximity, geographical dispersion has occurred on a massive scale. This reflects a shift in the carriers of globalization: while intra-industry trade dominated until the mid-1980s, since then, international production has grown considerably faster than international trade.[3] By the 1990s sales of foreign affiliates of multinational enterprises (MNEs) far outpaced exports as the principal vehicle to deliver goods and services to foreign markets.

It is important to emphasize that globalization should not be reduced to geographic dispersion. In contrast to the assumptions of the convergence theory, globalization does not lead to the wonderland of a 'borderless world' (Ohmae, 1991) where capital, knowledge and other resources move freely around the globe, acting as a powerful force of equalization.[4] *Globalization does not rescind the gravitational forces of geography.* It has given rise to 'ever more finely grained patterns of locational differentiation and specialisation' (Scott, 1998, p. 399). Inequality and diversity prevail. A breathtaking speed of geographical dispersion has been combined with spatial concentration: much of the recent cross-border extension of manufacturing and services has been concentrated on a handful of specialized local clusters, both within the Triad and some emerging economies, especially in East Asia.

The previous chapters on the Taiwanese SMEs and the electronics industry have offered interesting evidence of this. For instance the supply chain of a computer company typically spans different time zones and continents, and integrates a multitude of transactions and local clusters. The degree of dispersion differs across the value chain: it increases the closer one gets to the final product, while dispersion remains concentrated especially for critical precision components.

In short, rapid cross-border dispersion coexists with agglomeration. Globalization often occurs as an extension of national clusters across national borders. This implies two things: first, *some* stages of the value chain are internationally dispersed, while others remain concentrated; second, the internationally dispersed activities typically congregate in a limited number of overseas clusters. This clearly indicates that agglomeration economies continue to matter, as well as the path-dependent nature of the cluster evolution. What needs to be explained, however, is how they have changed under the impact of globalization. Concentrated dispersion thus raises an important question: what factors explain that some value-chain activities are more prone to geographical dispersion, while others are more prone to proximity constraints?

Much research on industrial restructuring has been based on a distinction between low-wage, low-skill sunset industries and high-wage, high-skill sunrise industries. The usual suspects of course are differences in labour costs and knowledge intensity. There is a strong presumption that high-wage and more knowledge-intensive activities are more prone to agglomeration effects, and hence resistant to geographical dispersion. By the same token, geographical dispersion can be expected to be most prominent for low-wage and low-skill value chain activities.

There is nothing surprising about these propositions (this is precisely what one would expect from an agglomeration economies perspective). This would seem to imply that a clear-cut separation is possible between low-end activities that are highly dispersed, and knowledge-intensive ones that require localized clusters.

Yet reality is considerably more messy. Any simple dichotomy has failed to produce convincing results, as shown in our book: first, there are low-wage, low-skill value stages even in the most high-tech industry, and high-wage, high-skill activities exist even in so-called traditional industries like textiles as pointed out in the chapters on the Italian industrial districts; second, both the capability requirements and the boundaries of a particular 'industry' keep changing over time, which makes an analytical focus on the industry level even more problematic.

An important complication results from the diversity of agglomeration propensities: co-location requirements differ across industries and product markets; they also differ across firms. These industry and firm-specific differences provide one possible explanation for the diversity of cluster development trajectories analysed in our book.

Take first industry-specific features: co-location becomes more important, the greater an industry's volatility, that is, the shorter its product life cycle (PLC), the quicker the required speed-to-market and the greater the number of design changes. Yet such co-location can occur at different places. This is borne out by the example of the hard disk drive (HDD) industry. Due to its high volatility, HDD assemblers cannot afford to have a geographically extended supply chain. Hence the importance for suppliers to locate close to the main drive assemblers (Ernst, 1997c; McKendrick *et al.*, 2000). During the early stages of this industry, this implied co-location at home (primarily around IBM's San José facility in California). We have seen that globalization has given rise to the concentrated international dispersion of such clusters.

Agglomeration propensities also differ by type of supplier.[5] For suppliers of standard equipment and components, there is no need for close interaction with their customers. However, intense interaction is essential for the client's relation with high-end suppliers of differentiated products that require proprietary technology. Paraphrasing price theory terminology, we call these suppliers *technology makers*.[6]

Intense localized interaction is necessary only for newly established and still relatively weak lower-tier suppliers (*technology takers*) who need to be nurtured until they can stand on their own feet. In the electronics industry, for instance, technology takers are frequently used as second sources. Their main purpose is to provide the client with a price leverage against suppliers who are technology setters and who are inclined to charge premium prices. Technology takers are also used as capacity buffers, especially when the technology setters resist client requests for price cuts. Divergent agglomeration propensities by type of supplier thus provides us with another differentiating factor that shapes distinct cluster development trajectories.

Probably the most important caveat to the agglomeration economies argument is that dispersion is no longer restricted to lower-end activities. The essential point is that distinctions should be made not on the basis of different industries, but rather for different value chain stages, and this notably applies also to more traditional sectors such as textiles and clothing. There is a growing literature that explains the bifurcation of geographical location patterns along functional activities (Audretsch and Feldman, 1996; McKendrick *et al.*, 2000) or value-chain stages (Dicken, 1992; Ernst, 1997c).

We now turn to an important organisational innovation, GPN, and its role as a carrier of international knowledge diffusion.

4. GLOBAL PRODUCTION NETWORKS AS CARRIERS OF KNOWLEDGE DIFFUSION

Geographical dispersion poses increasingly demanding co-ordination requirements. As pointed out in Ernst's chapter, global production networks are an organizational innovation that enables network flagships to combine concentrated dispersion with systemic forms of integration. These networks integrate the dispersed supply and customer bases of a network flagship, that is, its subsidiaries, affiliates and joint ventures, its suppliers and subcontractors, its distribution channels and value-added re-sellers, as well as its R&D alliances and a variety of co-operative agreements, such as standards consortia. The concept of GPNs may have some important implications also for the future evolution of the Italian industrial districts.

One reason to talk about systemic integration is the substantially broadened scope for international linkages: a GPN encompasses both intrafirm and inter-firm linkages; creates a diversity of network participants; links together multiple locations; and covers a variety of value chain stages, including higher-end, and more knowledge-intensive ones.

This raises a number of important issues that are highly contested in the literature. For instance, GPNs do not necessarily give rise to less hierarchical forms of firm organization (as predicted for instance in Bartlett and Ghoshal, 1989). Network participants differ in their access to and in their position within such networks, and hence face very different challenges. One could use a taxonomy of network participants that distinguishes various hierarchical layers that range from flagship companies that dominate such networks, down to a variety of usually smaller, local network participants (Ernst, 2000b). The flagship is at the heart of a network: it provides strategic and organizational leadership beyond the resources that, from an accounting perspective, lie directly under its management control (Rugman, 1997, p. 182).

The strategy of the flagship company thus directly affects the growth, the strategic direction and network position of lower-end participants, like specialized suppliers and subcontractors. The flagship derives its strength from its control over critical resources and capabilities, and from its capacity to co-ordinate transactions between the different network nodes. Both are the sources of its superior capacity for generating economic rents.[7] In the case of the industrial districts one could say that the flagship company has an equivalent that may be alternatively a leader or a hub performing a leadership role.

It is also important to distinguish the different capacities of firms to reap potential network benefits, and the institutions and policies required to support weaker network participants.

One critical capability, for instance, is the intellectual property and knowledge associated with setting, maintaining and continuously upgrading a de facto market standard. This requires perpetual improvements in product features, functionality, performance, cost and quality. It is such 'complementary assets' (Teece, 1986) that the flagship increasingly outsources. This has given rise to a number of organizational innovations that culminate in the spread of GPN. Take recent developments in the electronics industry which has become the most important breeding ground for a New Industrial Organization model (for example Chandler *et al.*, 1998). For instance, for a typical flagship in the PC business, the cost of components, software and services purchased from outside, has increased from less than 60 per cent to more than 80 per cent of total (ex factory) production costs (Ernst and O'Connor, 1992, chapter I). This has applied also to a lower technology sector such as textiles and clothing, even though to a much smaller extent. Here it is important to stress that the consequences of globalization on industrial restructuring and reorganization are going to be felt more and more across sectors in the future, and so the industry level could not be the relevant unit of analysis of such changes.

As external sourcing relations become geographically dispersed and increasingly complex, they are fraught with very high co-ordination costs: some firms report that the cost of co-ordinating such outside relations can exceed in-house manufacturing costs (see Chapter 5). As a result, the focus of cost reduction strategies is shifting from scale economies in manufacturing to a reduction of the cost of global sourcing.

In the electronics industry, as shown in our book, this has given rise to a proliferation of specialized suppliers, segmenting the industry into separate, yet closely interacting horizontal layers (Grove, 1996). Each of these individual market segments has become rapidly globalized. This has given rise to the co-existence of complex, globally organized sector-specific value chains, for instance for microprocessors, memories, PCs, HDD and other components, a process accelerated by the introduction of Internet-enabled virtual integration (Ernst, 2000c). Each of these value chains consists of a variety of GPNs that compete with each other, but that may also co-operate.

Most research on the location of knowledge-intensive activities has focused on the role of R&D, but this may be a too narrow focus (for details, see Ernst, 2000f). It is necessary to cast the net wider and to analyse the geographical dispersion of cross-functional, knowledge-intensive support services that are intrinsically linked with production. Even if these activities do not involve formal R&D, they may still give rise to considerable learning and innovation. The latter include for instance trial production (prototyping and ramping-up), tooling and equipment, benchmarking of productivity, testing, process adaptation, product customization and supply chain co-ordination. The result is that an increasing share of the value-added shifts across the boundaries of the firm as well as across national borders, as shown in the chapters on Taiwan's experience.

5. INTENSITY OF LINKAGES

Systemic integration also implies that international linkages are no longer secondary, quasi-optional to domestic linkages. Instead, existing clusters in any two countries supplement each other and may experience mutual inter-penetration.[8] Under such conditions international linkages are essential for the continuous growth of an industrial cluster.

This is self-evident for network suppliers, especially lower tier ones, whose growth and strategic direction is heavily determined by the network flagship or the industrial district leader. Dependence, however, also works the other way round. Insofar as that the flagship has moved to global sourcing, it may no longer have any credible domestic suppliers. This implies an erosion of the collective knowledge which used to be a characteristic feature of the flagship's home location. In some cases, that collective knowledge may have migrated for good to the supplier's overseas cluster(s).

This has important implications also for the experience of the Marshallian industrial districts and the high locally concentrated innovation capability that has been characterizing their evolution up to now.

The evolution of Silicon Valley provides a typical example of how the growing density of international knowledge linkages facilitates the continuous upgrading of an industrial cluster, providing new entry opportunities for small-scale start-up companies. This region has gone through various incarnations. Originally its main function was to churn out 'chips and computers', that is, to provide the basic inputs for the global electronics industry. Its economic structure was defined by a narrow product specialization, the incessant proliferation of new start-up companies, and disintegrated forms of firm organization: limited interaction within the firm between product development and production was compensated by a heavy reliance on the region's sophisticated knowledge base. Saxenian (1994a, p. 5), for instance, argues that, while the region's market orientation is global, its production and innovation system remains primarily local.

This distinction may have made sense during the early stages of development of the region; it is no longer valid. Today, Silicon Valley is a highly diversified industrial region that combines a handful of global network flagships with multiple layers of vibrant SMEs. Its growth is predicated on a capacity to connect and co-ordinate a variety of international linkages that cover almost all stages of the value chain, except hardcore R&D. This region now critically depends on its position as the source and control centre of a dense web of GPN that provide access to lower cost overseas supply bases, global labour markets for engineering talent and (potential) growth markets. Such international linkages can recharge local linkages. They provide important opportunities for international knowledge sourcing (a possible explanation for Silicon Valley's apparently inexhaustible upgrading capacity).[9]

6. NEW OPPORTUNITIES AND CHALLENGES FOR SME INDUSTRIAL CLUSTERS AND DISTRICTS

We have seen that the main purpose of new forms of industrial organization like GPNs is to gain quick access to lower cost foreign capabilities that are complementary to the flagship's own competencies. In order to mobilize and harness these external capabilities, flagships are forced to accept a certain dispersion of the value chain. They must also broaden their capability transfer to individual nodes of their GPN. The (often unintended) result is a creeping migration of knowledge to external actors abroad. This opens new opportunities for international knowledge linkages that SME-based industrial districts should strive to exploit. However it also raises complex challenges for policies as well as firm organization.

A GPN can create a virtuous circle of international knowledge diffusion for two main reasons. First, it increases the length of a firm's value chain, as well as its logistical complexity. This creates new gaps and interstices that can be addressed by small, specialized suppliers. While in some cases (like for instance 'screw-driver' contract assembly), such entry may be short-lived, this is not necessarily so. Outsourcing requirements have become more demanding and have forced specialized suppliers to develop their capabilities. Over time, they may be able to upgrade their position from simple contract manufacturers to providers of integrated service packages, and hence increase the benefits that they can reap from network participation.

Second, once a network supplier successfully upgrades its capabilities, this creates further pressure for a continuous migration of knowledge-intensive, higher value-added support activities to individual network nodes. This may also include engineering, product and process development, reflecting the increasingly demanding competitive requirements. In the electronics industry, for instance, product life-cycles have been cut to six months, and sometimes less, and speed-to-market is of the essence. Overseas production thus frequently occurs soon after the launching of new products. This is only possible if key design information is shared more freely between the network flagship and its overseas affiliates and suppliers. Speed-to-market requires that engineers across the different nodes of a GPN are plugged into the lead company's design debates (both on-line and face-to-face) on a regular basis.

All that may enhance the diffusion of knowledge across firm boundaries and national borders, and hence reshape the development trajectories of industrial clusters. Nothing is automatic, however, about these processes.

Integration into GPNs poses a fundamental challenge. An increased mobility of firm-specific resources and capabilities across national boundaries may erode established patterns of specialization, especially for smaller firms. It may also erode the strengths of existing clusters. This may increase the global divide between firms and districts that have and those that do not have access to the information and knowledge that is necessary to reap the benefits of network participation. Many people are understandably concerned that this may lead to a loss of competitiveness, and hence to a decline in growth and welfare.

There is, however, cause for cautious optimism: network participation may provide new opportunities for *reverse knowledge outsourcing* by SMEs and industrial districts. Our analysis has shown that GPNs are powerful vehicles for knowledge outsourcing across firm boundaries and national borders. It is important to emphasize their *dual* nature. Most debates focus on the strategic rationale underlying knowledge outsourcing by large global network flagship companies, and their organizational implications (for example, Patel and Pavitt, 1991; and Granstrand *et al.*, 1993). For SMEs, though, what matters is the other side of the coin: participation in GPNs can facilitate reverse knowledge outsourcing by smaller, lower-tier network participants that may help them to overcome some of their knowledge-related disadvantages.

Three effects of such reverse knowledge outsourcing can be distinguished. First, it can act as a conduit for knowledge transfers for state-of-the-art management approaches as well as product and process technologies. Second, at the same time, these international linkages can also act as catalysts for knowledge creation and capability development within both SMEs and their local environments. Third, over time these linkages may also give rise to joint knowledge creation, with roughly symmetrical contributions from the global network flagship and from the developing country network participants.

In our book we have demonstrated this process for Taiwanese computer firms. Their involvement in the OEM business, the most important of international linkages, has gone through different incarnations, from very simple arrangements to highly complex ones. Each of these stages has given rise to a peculiar pattern of knowledge outsourcing. Paradoxically, an increasing reliance on OEM arrangements has had positive effects for knowledge creation in Taiwan's computer industry. In contrast to a widespread perception (for example, Hobday, 1995), successful knowledge outsourcing does not necessarily require a sequential move from OEM, up to ODM, and then further up to OBM. Instead Taiwanese suppliers were able to learn and to create knowledge through *concurrent* implementation of these different knowledge outsourcing approaches.

It is important to emphasize the diversity of such linkages and their non-linear evolutionary character. International linkages include a variety of ties with sales, manufacturing and engineering support affiliates of foreign firms; they also include different forms and trajectories of integration into global production networks. Taiwanese firms, as shown in the book, have typically pursued different approaches in parallel, rather than concentrating exclusively on one particular linkage. It is through such concurrent and multiple linkages that a virtuous circle between knowledge outsourcing and knowledge creation becomes feasible. The Italian districts appear to share this tendency only to a minor extent, and a broadening of their linkages to reach out to distant foreign markets and actors such as large firms, flagship companies, and institutions appears desirable.

Reaping the benefits from participation in GPN cannot be left to market forces alone; much depends on the nature of supporting institutions and policies. An appropriate long-term perspective for the development of industrial districts must focus on improvements in specialization, productivity, and Hirschman-type linkages, all of which necessitate local capability formation and innovation. All these elements are essential prerequisites for improving the capacity to raise patient capital that is necessary for facility investment, R&D and welfare expenditures (Ernst, 2000e). As the example of small Nordic countries and the Netherlands demonstrates, the scope for proactive technology and industrial policies in a liberal ownership regime is far greater than commonly assumed. Taiwan, Singapore and recent developments in Korea also illustrate that a variety of approaches are possible to such policies, involving different interesting hybrid combinations. The choice is much larger than is normally assumed.

Implementing such policies, however, poses daunting political and administrative challenges. Supporting the restructuring process of an industrial cluster requires fundamental changes in the objectives and policy instruments, and a deep understanding of the global competitive dynamics. Not less, but actually more knowledge and expertise are required in the public sector. More specifically, developing a viable cluster requires a deep understanding of sector specificities, rather than a sector-neutral and minimally active policy stance. It requires an understanding of the widely varying technological properties of specific industries, the logistical and strategic concerns of multinational businesses, the fundamental transformations in the organization of their global production networks and the rapidly evolving international investment environment.

The real question, then, is no longer whether national and regional policies can make a difference. Instead, a critical challenge in a globalizing world is to develop a set of supporting institutions and policies that can foster local capability formation and innovation. That effort needs to be based on a sound understanding of how disruptive technological change and liberalization have changed the parameters of global competition, and hence the strategic options for developing SME-based local systems.

NOTES

1. For Krugman (1991a and b), agglomeration in essence results from three factors: (1) substantial *increasing* returns to scale – both at the level of the single firm (*internal* economies) and the industry (*external* economies); (2) sufficiently low transport costs; and (3) large local demand. Proximity matters, resulting in agglomeration, once these three factors interact. For an excellent critique of the 'New "Geographical" Turn in Economics',

see Martin (1999).

2.   After all, Marshall's analysis was shaped by value judgements which reflect a peculiar historical concern of the late 19th century Britain (Lazonick, 1999, p. 10 passim): Will Britain be able to survive the new and aggressive competition from emerging nations such as the US and Germany, with their highly concentrated industries? Marshall believed that 'a proliferation of small-scale proprietary enterprises was both a morally superior form of industrial organization and more favorable to economic development'. The implication was that economic development did not require concentrations of power within industry, like in the US and Germany.

3.   During the 1980s, FDI flows quadrupled, growing three times faster than trade flows, and almost four times faster than GDP. Growth has been less impressive, though, for FDI outward stock, which constitutes the capital base for MNE operations: it was 21 per cent between 1986 and 1990, (at current prices), fell to 10.3 per cent between 1991 and 1995, and increased again to 11.5 per cent (1996) and 13.7 per cent (1997) (UNCTAD, 1998, table I.1.).

4.   For a critique, see Boyer (1996) and Ernst and Ravenhill (1999).

5.   Williamson's concept of site specificity, a particular form of physical asset specificity, provides a formal treatment of this issue. A fundamental weakness, however, is the theory's inherent incapacity to address the issue of innovation. As Williamson himself explains: 'The introduction of innovation plainly complicates the earlier-described assignment of transactions to markets and hierarchies based entirely on an examination of their asset specificity qualities. Indeed, the study of economic organization in a regime of rapid innovation poses much more difficult issues than those addressed here' (1985, p. 143). In the final analysis, Williamson's theory explains the firm as a response to market failure: 'The cause of this market failure is "asset specificity" – a technological condition that is given to the firm' (Lazonick, 1999, p. 22).

6.   Price theory distinguishes perfect competition, where the firm is a price *taker*, that is, it has no choice but to accept the price that has been determined in the market, and monopolistic competition, where the monopolist can, if so inclined, raise his price (price maker). In analogy, we distinguish technology *makers* that possess proprietary technology and hence can shape the design trajectory of a particular product or service, and technology *takers* that have no choice but to accept the design principles established by the former.

7.   I refer of course to Penrose-type rents. Spender (1998, p. 433) demonstrates that 'each type of knowledge can, in principle, be associated with a different kind of rent and competitive advantage'. Tacit social knowledge (which Spender calls *collective*) is of critical importance: 'The collective knowledge which develops as key players interact under conditions of uncertainty leads to Penrose rents, so labelled because such activity-based learning lies at the core of her theory of the growth of the firm'.

8.   *Partial* integration is characterized by a loose patchwork of arms' length trade and stand-alone, unrelated investment projects. Most of these focus either on access to domestic markets or on exploiting particular resources (cheap labour). They are *footloose*, in the sense that they are prone to rapid closure and redeployment. Partial integration implies a limited scope for international specialization. This is due to an absence of interactions across functions and locations, and to a lack of co-ordination.

9.   The critical importance of international linkages is also reflected in the new research agenda of AnnaLee Saxenian whose earlier work on informal peer group networks in Silicon Valley (Saxenian, 1994) made an important contribution to the debate on localized agglomeration economies. She has now moved on to study *international* linkages: the dense links between the Valley and Taiwan, India, and China, through trans-national technical communities, especially circuit designers and computer engineers (Saxenian, 1999). For a case study of how Taiwan's computer industry has benefited from such international knowledge linkages, see Ernst (2000d).

Bibliography

Acs, Z.J. and D.B. Audretsch (1992), *Innovation and Small Firms*, Cambridge MA: The MIT Press.

Albino, A., P. Garavelli and F. Pontrandolfo (1996), 'Local Factors and Global Strategies of the Leader Firm of an Industrial District', paper presented at EurOMA Conference on Manufacturing Strategy, London, June.

Andersen, E.S. (1996), 'The Evolution of Economic Complexity: A Division-of-Coordination-of Labor Approach', in E. Helmstaedter and M. Perlman (eds), *Behavioral Norms, Technological Progress, and Economic Dynamics. Studies in Schumpeterian Economics*, Ann Arbor: The University of Michigan Press.

Antonelli, C. (1999), *The Microdynamics of Technological Knowledge*, Italy: Dipartimento di Economia, Universita di Torino.

Antonelli, C. and R. Marchionatti (1998), 'Technological and Organisational Change in a Process of Industrial Rejuvenation: the Case of the Italian Cotton Textile Industry', *Cambridge Journal of Economics*, 22 (1), pp. 1-18.

Archibugi, D. (2000), 'The Globalisation of Technology and The European Innovation System', paper presented at DRUID Conference, University of Aalborg, June.

Archibugi, D. and S. Iammarino (1998), 'The Policy Implications of the Globalisation of Technology', *Research Policy*, 28 (2-3), pp. 317-36.

Archibugi, D. and J. Michie (1995), 'The Globalization of Technology: A New Taxonomy', *Cambridge Journal of Economics*, 19 (1).

Archibugi, D. and J. Michie (1997), *Technology, Globalisation and Economic Performance*, Cambridge: Cambridge University Press.

Asheim, B.T. (1996), 'Industrial Districts as "Learning Regions": a

Condition for Prosperity', *European Planning Studies*, 4 (4), pp. 379-400.

Asia IT Report, monthly, Market Intelligence Centre, Institute for Information Industry, Taipei, Taiwan.

Audretsch, D.B. and M.P. Feldman (1996), 'R&D Spillovers and the Geography of Innovation and Production', *American Economic Review*, 86, pp. 630-40.

Aw, Bee Yan, Xiaomin Chen and J. Roberts Mark (1997), 'Firm-level Evidence on Productivity Differentials, Turnover, and Exports in Taiwanese Manufacturing', NBER Working Paper No. 6235, pp. 1-25.

Badaracco, J.L. (1991), *The Knowledge Link: How Firms Compete through Strategic Alliances*, Boston, MA: Harvard Business School Press.

Bagella, M. (ed.) (1996), *Internazionalizzazione della Piccola e Media Impresa in America Latina*, Bologna, Italy: Il Mulino.

Bagella, M. and C. Pietrobelli (1995), 'Distretti industriali e internalizzazione: presupposti teorici ed evidenza empirica dall'America latina', *Economia e politica industriale*, 86, pp. 69-93.

Bagella, M. and C. Pietrobelli (1997), 'From SMEs to Industrial Districts in the Process of Internationalization: Theory and Evidence', in M.P. van Dijk and R. Rabellotti (eds), *Enterprise Clusters and Networks in Developing Countries*, London: Frank Cass.

Baptista, R. and P. Swann (1998), 'Do Firms in Clusters Innovate More?', *Research Policy*, 27, pp. 525-40.

Barca, F. and M. Magnani (1989), *L'industria fra capitale e lavoro*, Bologna, Italy: Il Mulino.

Bartlett, C.A. and S. Ghoshal (eds) (1989), *Managing Across Borders: The Transnational Solution*, London: Century Business.

Becattini, G. (ed.) (1987), *Mercato e forze locali: il distretto industriale*, Bologna, Italy: Il Mulino.

Becattini, G. (1990), 'The Marshallian Industrial District as a Socio-economic Notion', in F. Pyke, G. Becattini and W. Senbenberger (eds),

Industrial Districts and Inter-firm Co-operation in Italy, Geneva: International Institute for Labour Studies.

Becattini, G. (1995), *I sistemi locali come strumento interpretativo dello sviluppo italiano*, Florence, Italy: IRIS.

Becchetti, L. and S. Rossi (1998), 'The Positive Effect of Industrial District on the Export Performance of Italian Firms', Italy: University of Tor Vergata, CEIS Working Paper No. 54.

Bell, Martin and Keith Pavitt (1993), 'Technological Accumulation and Industrial Growth: Contrasts Between Developed and Developing Countries', *Industrial and Corporate Change*, 2 (2).

Bellandi, M. (1996), 'Innovation and Change in the Marshallian Industrial District', *European Planning Studies*, 4 (3).

Belussi, F. and F. Arcangeli (1998), 'A Typology of Networks: Flexible and Evolutionary Firms', *Research Policy*, 27, pp. 415-28.

Borrus, M., D. Ernst and S. Haggard (eds) (2000), *International Production Networks in Asia: Rivalry or Riches?*, London: Routledge.

Boyer, R. (1996), 'The Convergence Hypothesis Revisited: Globalization but Still the Century of Nations?', in S. Berger and R. Dore (eds), *National Diversity and Global Capitalism*, Ithaca and London: Cornell University Press.

Bresnahan, Timothy and Franco Malerba (1997), 'Industrial Dynamics and the Evolution of Firms' and Nations' Competitive Capabilities in the World Computer Industry', paper presented to the DRUID seminar on Industrial Dynamics and Competition, June, Skagen, Denmark.

Brezis, E.S. and P. Krugman (1993), 'Technology and the Life Cycle of Cities', NBER Working Paper No. 4561.

Brusco, S. and S. Paba (1997), 'Per una storia dei distretti industriali italiani dal secondo dopoguerra agli anni novanta', in F. Barca (ed.), *Storia del capitalismo italiano dal dopoguerra a oggi*, Rome: Donzelli Editore.

Bursi, T., G. Marchi and G. Pappalardo (1997), *Indagine sulle condizioni economico-finanziarie delle imprese emiliano-romagnole del tessile abbigliamento (1994-96)*, Banca Popolare dell'Emilia Romagna e CITER Carpi.

Bursi, T., G. Nardin and G. Pappalardo (1996), *Indagine sulle condizioni economico-finanziarie delle imprese emiliano-romagnole del tessile abbigliamento (1993-95)*, Banca Popolare dell'Emilia Romagna e CITER Carpi.

Callon, S. (1994), 'Different Paths: The Rise of Taiwan and Singapore in the Global Personal Computer Industry', Japan Development Bank Discussion Paper Series No. 9404, Tokyo.

Camagni, R. (1997), 'I milieux di alta tecnologia in Italia e nuove riflessioni sul concetto di milieu innovateur', mimeo, University of Padua.

Cantwell, J.A. (ed.) (1994), *Transnational Corporations and Innovatory Activities*, London: Routledge.

Cantwell, J.A. and S. Iammarino (1998), 'MNCs, Technological Innovation and Regional Systems in the EU: Some Evidence in the Italian Case', *International Journal of the Economics of Business*, Special Issue, 5 (3), pp. 383-408.

Cantwell, J.A. and S. Iammarino (2000), 'Multinational Corporations and the Location of Technological Innovation in the UK Regions', *Regional Studies*, 34 (3), pp. 317-22.

Cantwell, J.A. and S. Iammarino (2001), 'Regional Systems of Innovation in Europe and the Globalisation of Technology', in A. Bartzokas (eds), *Technology Policy and Regional Integration*, London: Routledge, forthcoming.

Capello, R. (1999), 'Spatial Transfer of Knowledge in High-technology Milieux: Learning vs. Collective Learning Processes', *Regional Studies*, 33 (4), pp. 353-65.

Carlsson, B. and R. Stankiewicz (1991), 'On the Nature, Function and Composition of Technological Systems', *Journal of Evolutionary Economics*, 1 (2).

Carminucci, C. and S. Casucci (1997), 'Il ciclo di vita dei distretti industriali: ipotesi teoriche ed evidenze empiriche', *L'Industria*, XVIII (2), pp. 283-315.

Castellano, F. (1999), 'Distritos Industriales y Modelos Organizativos de Pymes', Masters Thesis, EU-ALFA Programme, Italy: Rome University, Tor Vergata.

Castells, M. (1998), *The Information Age*, 3 volumes, London: Blackwell.

Caves, R.E. (1982), *Multinational Enterprise and Economic Analysis*, Cambridge: Cambridge University Press.

Censis (1997), 'VIII Forum Nazionale dei Localismi. Distretti industriali e sviluppo economico locale', in *CENSIS Note e Commenti*, XXXIII (9), September.

Censis (1998), 'VIII Forum Nazionale dei Localismi. Distretti industriali, infrastrutture e servizi per la logistica', in *CENSIS Note e Commenti*.

Chandler, A. (1990), *Scale and Scope: The Dynamics of Industrial Capitalism*, Cambridge, MA: Belknap Press.

Chandler, A.D. *et al.* (eds) (1998), *The Dynamic Firm. The Role of Technology, Strategy, Organization, and Regions*, Oxford: Oxford University Press.

Chen, G.S. (1993), *Coordinating Network and Life Structure – Socio-economic Analysis of Taiwan's Small and Medium Enterprises* (in Chinese), Taipei: United Economic Publishers.

Chen, Tain-Jy *et al.* (1995), *Taiwan's Small and Medium-Sized Firms' Direct Investment in Southeast Asia*, Taipei: Chung-Hua Institution for Economic Research.

Christensen, Jens F. (1996), 'Innovative Assets and Inter-asset Linkages – A Resource-based Approach to Innovation', *Economics of Innovation and New Technology*, 4, pp. 193-209.

Ciciotti, E. (1993), *Competitività e territorio. L'economia regionale nei paesi industrializzati*, Rome, Italy: La Nuova Italia Scientifica.

Conti, G. (1994), 'I sistemi esportativi italiani: un'analisi per province 1985-1993', *Rapporto ICE*, pp. 251-67.

Conti, G. and S. Menghinello (1995), 'Territorio e competitività:

l'importanza dei sistemi locali per le esportazioni italiane di manufatti. Un'analisi per province 1985-1993', *Rapporto ICE*, pp. 286-303.

Conti, G. and S. Menghinello (1996), 'L'internazionalizzazione produttiva dei "sistemi locali"', *Rapporto ICE*, Chapter 7.

Conti, G. and S. Menghinello (2000), 'Competitività e dimensione locale: alcune riflessioni sulla base di una nuova evidenza empirica', *Rapporto ICE-Istat* 1999-2000, pp. 205-14.

Cox, K.R. (ed.) (1997), *Spaces and Globalisation: Reasserting the Power of the Local*, New York: Guilford.

Dahlman, C., B. Ross-Larson and L. Westphal (1987), 'Managing Technological Development: Lessons from the Newly Industrialising Countries', *World Development*, 15 (6).

Dicken, P. (1992), *Global Shift.Transforming the World Economy*, 2nd edn, London: Paul Chapman Publishing.

Dicken, P. (1994) 'The Roepke Lecture in Economic Geography. Global-Local Tensions: Firms and States in the Global Space Economy', *Economic Geography*, 70 (2), pp. 101-28.

Dicken, P. and P.E. Lloyd (1990), *Location in Space. Theoretical Perspectives in Economic Geography*, 3rd edn, New York: HarperCollins.

Dosi, Giovanni, Christopher Freeman, Richard Nelson, Gerald Silverberg and Luc Soete (eds) (1988), *Technical Change and Economic Theory*, London: Pinter.

Dunning, J.H. (1993), *Multinational Enterprises and the Global Economy*. Wokingham: Addison-Wesley.

Dunning, J.H. (1998), 'Globalization, Technology and Space', in A.D. Chandler *et al.* (eds), *The Dynamic Firm. The Role of Technology, Strategy, Organization, and Regions*, Oxford: Oxford University Press.

Enright, M. (1998), 'Regional Clusters and Firm Strategy', in A.D. Chandler *et al.* (eds), *The Dynamic Firm. The Role of Technology, Strategy, Organization, and Regions*, Oxford: Oxford University Press.

Ernst, D. (1983), *The Global Race in Microelectronics*, with a foreword by David Noble, Frankfurt and New York: MIT, Campus Publishers.

Ernst, D. (1994a), *What are the Limits to the Korean Model? The Korean Electronics Industry Under Pressure*, A BRIE Research Monograph, The Berkeley Roundtable on the International Economy, University of California at Berkeley.

Ernst, D. (1994b), 'Network Transactions, Market Structure and Technological Diffusion – Implications for South-South Cooperation', in L. Mytelka (ed.), *South-South Cooperation in a Global Perspective*, Development Centre Documents, Paris: OECD.

Ernst, D. (1997a), 'High-tech Competition Puzzles. How Globalization Affects Firm Behavior and Market Structure in the Electronics Industry', Danish Research Unit for Industrial Dynamics (DRUID) Working Paper No. 97-10, September.

Ernst, D. (1997b), 'Partners in the China Circle? The Asian Production Networks of Japanese Electronics Firms', in Barry Naughton (ed.), *The China Circle*, Washington, DC: The Brookings Institution Press.

Ernst, D. (1997c), 'From Partial to Systemic Globalization. International Production Networks in the Electronics Industry', *BRIE Working Paper No. 98*, the Berkeley Roundtable on the International Economy (BRIE), University of California at Berkeley, April.

Ernst, D. (1997d), 'Catching-up, Crisis and Industrial Upgrading: Evolutionary Aspects of Technology Management in Korea's Electronics Industry', to appear in *Asia-Pacific Journal of Management*.

Ernst, D. (1997e), 'International Production Networks and Local Capabilities. How Globalization Affects Industrial Upgrading Strategies', paper prepared for the Social Science Research Council (SSRC), New York, September.

Ernst, D. (1998), 'High-tech Competition Puzzles. How Globalization Affects Firm Behavior and Market Structure in the Electronics Industry', *Revue d'Economie Industrielle*, 85.

Ernst, D. (2000a) (forthcoming), 'The Economics of Electronics Industry: Competitive Dynamics and Industrial Organization', in *The International Encyclopedia of Business and Management* (IEBM), Malcolm Warner and

William Lazonick (eds).

Ernst, D. (2000b) (forthcoming), 'Globalization and the Changing Geography of Innovation Systems. A Policy Perspective on Global Production Networks', special issue of the *Journal of the Economics of Innovation and New Technologies*, on 'Integrating Policy Perspectives in Research on Technology and Economic Growth', edited by Anthony Bartzokas and Morris Teubal.

Ernst, D. (2000c), 'Placing the Networks on the Web. Challenges and Opportunities for Managing in Developing Asia', paper presented at the Second Asia Academy of Management Conference 'Managing in Asia: Challenges and Opportunities in the New Millenium', December 15-18, 2000, Shangri-La Hotel, Singapore.

Ernst, D. (2000d), 'Globalization, Information Technology and Industrial Upgrading – A Knowledge-centered Conceptual Framework', paper prepared for SSRC working group meeting on industrial upgrading, San Jose, Costa Rica, October 12-14, 2000.

Ernst, D. (2000e) (forthcoming), 'The Internationalization of Knowledge Support Functions: Global Production Networks in Information Industries', *Research Policy*.

Ernst, D., T. Ganiatsos and L. Mytelka (eds) (1998), *Technological Capabilities and Export Success – Lessons from East Asia*, London: Routledge Press.

Ernst D. and P. Guerrieri (1998), 'International Production Networks and Changing Trade Patterns in East Asia: The Case of the Electronics Industry', *Oxford Development Studies*, 26 (2).

Ernst, D. and B.-Å. Lundvall (1997/1998), 'Information Technology in The Learning Economy – Challenges for Developing Countries', Danish Research Unit for Industrial Dynamics (DRUID) Working Paper No. 97-12, Department of Business Studies, Aalborg University, Denmark. Revised version in Erich Reinert (ed.) (1998), *Evolutionary Economics and Spatial Income Inequality*, London: Edward Elgar Press.

Ernst, D. and D. O'Connor (1989), *Technology and Global Competition. The Challenge for Newly Industrialising Economies*, OECD Development Centre Studies, Paris: OECD.

Ernst, D. and D. O'Connor (1992), *Competing in the Electronics Industry. The Experience of Newly Industrialising Economies*, Development Centre Studies, Paris: OECD.

Ernst, D. and J. Ravenhill (1999), 'Globalization, Convergence, and the Transformation of International Production Networks in Electronics in East Asia', *Business & Politics*, 1 (1), University of California at Berkeley.

Esposito, G.F. (1994), 'Impresa e mercato: alcune ipotesi interpretative sulle dinamiche evolutive dei distretti industriali', Istituto Guglielmo Tagliacarne Working Paper 1.94.

Esposito, G.F. and D. Mauriello (1996), 'Subcontracting Systems and Organizational Changes in Italian Industrial Districts', Istituto Guglielmo Tagliacarne Working Paper 8.96.

Eurostat (1998), *European Union Direct Investment*, Yearbook 1997, Luxembourg EC.

Ferguson, C.H. (1990), 'Computers and the Coming of the U.S. Keiretsu', *Harvard Business Review*, July-August.

Fields, K.J. (1995), *Enterprise and the State in Korea and Taiwan*, Ithaca: Cornell University Press.

Flamm, K. (1988), *Creating the Computer. Government, Industry and High Technology*, Washington, DC: The Brookings Institution.

Flamm, K. (1990), 'Cooperation and Competition in the Global Computer Industry', paper prepared for the working group meeting on the 'Globalisation in the Computer Industry', OECD, Paris, December.

Foray, D. and B.-Å. Lundvall (1996), 'The Knowledge-based Economy: From the Economics of Knowledge to the Learning Economy', in OECD, *Employment and Growth in the Knowledge-based Economy*, OECD Documents, Paris: OECD.

Foss, N.J. (1993), 'Theories of the Firm: Competence and Contractual Perspectives', *Journal of Evolutionary Economics*, 3, pp. 127-44.

Foss, N.J. (1996), 'Capabilities and the Theory of the Firm', DRUID Working Paper No. 96-8, Department of Industrial Economics and Strategy,

Copenhagen Business School, June.

Foss, N.J. and C. Knudsen (eds) (1996), *Towards a Competence Theory of the Firm*, London: Routledge.

Freeman, C. (1982), *The Economics of Industrial Innovation*, London: Pinter.

Freeman, C. and B.-Å. Lundvall (eds) (1988), *Small Countries Facing the Technological Revolution*, London: Pinter.

Frova, S. (ed.) (1996), *L'industria meccanotessile in Italia. Comportamenti strategici, commerciali, finanziari*, Milan: EGEA.

Garofoli, G. (1991), *Modelli locali di sviluppo*, Milan: Franco Angeli.

Gobbo, F. (ed.) (1989), *Distretti e sistemi produttivi alla soglia degli anni '90*, Milan: Franco Angeli.

Gold, T.B. (1986), *State and Society in the Taiwan Miracle*, Armonk, New York and London: M.E. Sharpe, Inc.

Granstrand, O., L. Håkanson and S. Sjoelander (1993), 'Internationalization of R&D – A Survey of Some Recent Research', *Research Policy*, 22.

Grassi, M. and R. Pagni (1998), 'Sistemi Produttivi Localizzati e Imprese Leader', *IRPET, Interventi, Note e Rassegne*, Florence.

Gray M., E. Golob and A. Markusen (1996), 'Big Firms, Long Arms, Wide Shoulders: The "Hub-and-Spoke" Industrial District in the Seattle Region', *Regional Studies*, 30 (7).

Grossman, G.M. and E. Helpman (1991), *Innovation and Growth in the Global Economy*, The MIT Press, Cambridge, MA.

Grossman, G.M. and E. Helpman (1993), 'Endogenous Innovation in the Theory of Growth', working paper No. 4527, National Bureau of Economic Research (NBER), Cambridge, MA.

Grove, A.S. (1996), *Only the Paranoid Survive. How to Exploit the Crisis Points that Challenge Every Company and Career*, New York and London: HarperCollins Business.

Guerrieri, P. (1999a), 'Il commercio estero', Chap. 2 in S. Ferrari *et al.* (eds), *L'Italia nella competizione tecnologica internazionale. Secondo Rapporto*, Milan: FrancoAngeli.

Guerrieri, P. (1999b), 'Patterns of national specialisations in the Global Competitive Environment' in D. Archibugi, C.J. Howells and J. Nichie (eds), *Innovation Policy in a Global Economy*, Cambridge: Cambridge University Press.

Guerrieri P., S. Iammarino and C. Pietrobelli (1998), 'Agglomeration Economies, Cluster Effects and Industrial Districts: A Survey of the Literature', mimeo for EU-TSER, Rome: Institute for International Affairs.

Guerrieri, P. and Tylecote (1997), 'Inter-industry Differences in Technological Change and National Patterns of Technological Accumulation', in C. Edquist (ed.), *Systems of Innovation*, London and Washington, DC: Pinter Publishers.

Hagedoorn, J., A.N. Link and N.S. Vonortas (2000), 'Research Partnerships', *Research Policy*, 29, pp. 567-86.

Harman, T. (1971), *The International Computer Industry: Innovation and Comparative Advantage*, Cambridge, MA: Harvard University Press.

Harrison, B. (1994), *Lean and Mean. The Changing Landscape of Corporate Power in the Age of Flexibility*, New York: Basic Books.

Hobday, M. (1995), *Innovation in East Asia: The Challenge to Japan*, Aldershot: Edward Elgar.

Hu, Ming-Wen and Chi Schive (1998), 'The Changing Competitiveness of Taiwan's Manufacturing SMEs', *Small Business Economics*, pp. 1-12.

Humphrey, J. (1995), 'Industrial Reorganization in Developing Countries: From Models to Trajectories', *World Development*, 23 (1), pp. 149-62.

Hymer, S.H. (1960/1976), *The International Operations of National Firms: A Study of Direct Investment*, Cambridge, MA: MIT Press.

ICE (1998), *Rapporto sul commercio estero 1997*, Rome.

IDSE-CNR (1999), *Trasformazioni Strutturali e Competitività dei Sistemi*

Locali di Produzione, Milan: Franco Angeli.

Istat (1997), *I sistemi locali del lavoro 1991*, Rome.

Istat (1998), *Annuari di contabilità nazionale*, Rome.

Istituto Guglielmo Tagliacarne and Unioncamere (1997), *Rapporto 1996 sull'impresa e le economie locali*, Milan: Franco Angeli.

Johnson, C. (1987), 'Political Institutions and Economic Performance: The Government-Business Relationship in Japan, South Korea and Taiwan', in F.C. Deyo (ed.), *The Political Economy of the New Asian Industrialization*, Ithaca, NY: Cornell University Press.

Jolly, V.K. and K.A. Bechler (1992), 'Logitech: The Mouse that Roared', *Planning Review*, 20 (6), pp. 20-48.

Kajiwara, H. (1993), 'Taiwan's Electronics Industry: From an Import Substitution and Export Oriented Industry to a Highly Advanced Industry', in R. Inoue *et al.* (eds), *Industrial Policy in East Asia*, Tokyo: JETRO.

Kim Linsu (1997), *Imitation to Innovation. The Dynamics of Korea's Technological Learning*, Boston, MA: Harvard Business School Press.

Kline, S.J. and N. Rosenberg (1986), 'An Overview of Innovation', in R. Landau and N. Rosenberg (eds), *The Positive Sum Strategy*, Washington, DC: National Academy Press.

Knorringa, P. (1998), 'Cluster Trajectories in Developing Countries. Towards a Typology', paper presented at the EADI Workshop at the Institute of Social Studies, The Hague, 18-19 September.

Kobayashi, S. (1995), 'Current Situation of Taiwan's Economy and Future Issues', *Pacific Business and Industries*, III, (29), Center for Pacific Business Studies, Sakura Institute of Research, Tokyo.

Kogut, B. and E. Zander (1993), 'Knowledge of the Firm and the Evolutionary Theory of the Multinational Corporation', *Journal of International Business Studies*, 24 (4).

Kotler, P. *et al.*, (1985), *The New Competition. Meeting the Marketing Challenge from the Far East*, Englewood Cliffs, NJ: Prentice Hall

International.

Kraemer, K.L., J. Dedrick, Chi-Yeong Hwang, Tze-Chen Tu and Chee-Sing Yap (1996), 'Entrepreneurship, Flexibility, and Policy Coordination: Taiwan Computer Industry', *The Information Society*, 12, pp. 215-49.

Krugman, P. (1991a), *Geography and Trade*, Cambridge, MA: MIT Press.

Krugman, P. (1991b), 'History and Industry Location: The Case of Manufacturing Belt', *American Economic Review*, 81 (2), pp. 80-83.

Krugman, P. (1995), *Development, Geography and Economic Theory*, Cambridge, MA: MIT Press.

Kuo, W.J. (1998), *White Paper on Small and Medium Enterprises*, Taipei: Small Business Administration, Ministry of Economic Affairs.

Lai, J.C. (1998), 'The Competitive and Survival Strength of Small and Medium Enterprises – An Empirical Study of Taiwan's Electronics and Electrical Firms' (in Chinese), third Academic Conference for the Development of SMEs, Taipei: Small Business Administration, Ministry of Economic Affairs.

Lall, S. (1990), *Building Industrial Competitiveness in Developing Countries*, OECD Development Centre Studies, Paris: OECD.

Lall, S. (1997), 'Technological Change and Industrialization in the Asian NIEs: Achievements and Challenges', paper presented at international symposium on 'Innovation and Competitiveness in Newly Industrializing Economies', Science & Technology Policy Institute, Seoul, Korea, May 26-27.

Lall, S. and C. Pietrobelli (2001), *Failing to Compete: Technology Development and Technology Systems in Africa*, Cheltenham, UK and Lyme, US: Edward Elgar, forthcoming.

Lam, D.K.K. and I. Lee (1992), 'Guerrilla Capaitalism and the Limits of Static Theory: Comparing the Chinese NICs', in C. Clark and S. Chan (eds), *The Evolving Pacific Basin in the Global Political Economy. Domestic and International Linkages*, Boulder & London: Lynne Rienner Publishers.

Langlois, R.N. (1992), 'External Economies and Economic Progress: The

Case of the Microcomputer Industry', *Business History Review*, 66, Spring.

Langlois, R.N. and P.L. Robertson (1995), *Firms, Markets and Economic Change: A Dynamic Theory of Business Institutions*, London: Routledge.

Langlois, R.N. and W. Edward Steinmueller (1997), 'The Evolution of Competitive Advantage in the Global Semicondcutor Industry: 1947-1996', paper presented to the DRUID seminar on Industrial Dynamics and Competition, June, Skagen, Denmark.

Lazonick, W. (1999), 'Innovative Enterprise in Theory and History', INSEAD, March.

Lee, C.J. (1995), 'The Industrial Networks of Taiwanese SMEs', manuscript, Chung-Hua Institution for Economic Research, Taipei, Taiwan.

Lee, C.J. and Chi-Keung Li (1994), *APEC Survey on Small and Medium Enterprises*, APEC Secretariat, December.

Lee, H.L. and C. Billington (1995), 'The Evolution of Supply-chain Management Models and Practice at Hewlett Packard', *Interface*, 25 (5), September-October.

Lee, J.F. and Y.J. Yu (1996), 'A Study on the Relationship between Taiwan's Manufacturing Network and Technological Development' (in Chinese), Conference on Technology and Industrial Networks, Taipei, National Cheng-Chi University, 25 September.

Levy, D. (1995), 'International Sourcing and Supply Chain Stability', *Journal of International Business Studies*, second quarter.

Lim, L. and Pang Eng Fong (1991), *Foreign Direct Investment and Industrialisation in Malaysia, Singapore, Taiwan and Thailand*, OECD Development Centre Study, Paris: OECD.

Liu, C.Y. (1993), 'Government's Role in Developing a High-tech Industry: The Case of Taiwan's Semiconductor Industry', *Technovation*, 13 (5).

Liu, J., T. Luo and A. Weng (1995), *Semiconductor Industry Update 1995*, Taipei: Corporate Banking Group, Citibank.

Liu, P.C., Y.C. Liu and H.L. Wu (1994), 'Emergence of New Business

Organization and Management in Taiwan', *Industry of Free China*, Taipei, November.

Liu, Z.J. (1997), *Restructuring Taiwan's Industrial Competitiveness* (in Chinese), Taipei: Yuan Lin Publishing Co.

Llerena, P. and E. Zuscovitch (1996), 'Innovation, Diversity and Organization from an Evolutionary Perspective – Introduction and Overview', *Economics of Innovation and New Technology*, 4 (2).

Lorenzoni, G. (1990), *L'architettura di sviluppo delle imprese minori*, Bologna: Il Mulino.

Luethje, B. (1999), *Produktionsstrategien, Zulieferernetze und Arbeitsbeziehungen in der EDV-Industrie des 'Silicon Valley'* (Production Strategies, Subcontractor Networks and Labor Relations in the Computer Industry of Silicon Valley), Frankfurt am main: Habilitation, Department of Social Science, Johann Wolfgang Goethe-Universitaet.

Lundvall, B.-Å. (1988), 'Innovation as an Interactive Process: From User-Producer Interaction to the National System of Innovation', in G. Dosi *et al.* (eds), *Technical Change and Economic Theory*, London: Pinter Publishers.

Lundvall, B.-Å. (ed.) (1992), *National Systems of Innovation: Towards a Theory of Innovation and Interactive Learning*, London: Pinter Publishers.

Lundvall, B.-Å. (1996), 'The Social Dimension of the Learning Economy', DRUID Working Paper, No. 1, April, Department of Business Studies, Aalborg University.

Magaziner, I. and M. Patinkin (1989), 'Fast Heat: How Korea Won the Microwave War', *Harvard Business Review*, January-February.

Malerba, F. and G. Gavetti (1996), 'Il sistema innovativo italiano e L'Europa', *Economia e Politica Industriale,* 89, pp. 231-60.

Malerba, F. and L. Orsenigo (1995a), 'Schumpeterian Patterns of Innovation', *Cambridge Journal of Economics*, 19, pp. 47-65.

Malerba, F. and L. Orsenigo (1995b), 'Technological Innovation and International Competitiveness in Italy', in J. Molero (ed.), *Technological Innovation, multinational corporations and new international competitiveness*, Reading: Harwood Academic Publishers.

Malerba, F. and L. Orsenigo (1996a), 'The Dynamics and Evolution of Firms', *Industrial and Corporate Change*, 5 (1).

Malerba, F. and L. Orsenigo (1996b), 'Schumpeterian Patterns of Innovation are Technology-specific', *Research Policy*, 25, pp. 451-78.

Markusen, A. (1996a), 'Sticky Places in Slippery Space: A Typology of Industrial Districts', *Economic Geography*, 72, pp. 293-313.

Markusen, A. (1996b), 'Big Firms, Long Arms, Wide Shoulders: The "Hub-and-Spoke" Industrial District in the Seattle Region', *Regional Studies*, 30 (7), pp. 651-66.

Marshall, A. (1891), *Principles of Economics*, 2nd edn, London: Macmillan.

Marshall, A. (1896), *Principles of Economics*, London: Macmillan.

Marshall, A. (1890/1916), *Principles of Economics: An Introductory Volume*, 7th edn, London: Macmillan.

Martin, R. (1999), 'New Geographical Turn in Economics', *Cambridge Journal of Economics*, January.

Maskell, P. (1996a), 'Learning in the Village Economy of Denmark. The Role of Institutions and Policy in Sustaining Competitiveness', DRUID Working Paper No. 96-6, Department of Industrial Economics and Strategy, Copenhagen Business School, May.

Maskell, P. (1996b), 'The Process and Consequences of Ubiquification', paper prepared for the DRUID workshop, January 1997, Department of Industrial Economics and Strategy, Copenhagen Business School.

McKendrick, D., R. Doner and S. Haggard (2000), *From Silicon Valley to Singapore: Location and Competitive Advantage in the Hard Disk Drive Industry*, San Diego: Information Storage Industry Center, University of California.

Meaney, C.S. (1994), 'State Policy and the Development of Taiwan's Semiconductor Industry', in J.D. Auerbach *et al.* (eds), *The Role of the State in Taiwan's Development*, Armonk, New York, London: M.E. Sharpe.

Milgrom, P. and J. Roberts (1992), *Economics, Organization and Management*, Englewood Cliffs, NJ: Prentice Hall International.

Miner, A.S. and P.S. Haunschild (1995), 'Population Level Learning', *Research in Organizational Behavior*, 17, pp. 115-66.

Ministry of Economic Affairs (MOEA) (1991), *Small and Medium Enterprises White Paper*, Taipei, Taiwan.

Moda Industria (1997a), 'Commercio estero 1996', *Moda Consult*, Milan.

Moda Industria (1997b), 'Rapporto di settore 1996', *Moda Consult*, Milan.

Moda Industria (1998), 'Commercio estero. Abbigliamento, maglieria e calzetteria', no. 4, *Moda Consult*, Milan.

Nelson, R. (ed.) (1992), *National Innovation Systems*, London etc.: Oxford University Press.

Nelson, R. and H. Pack (1995), 'The Asian Growth Miracle and Modern Growth Theory', manuscript, School of International and Public Affairs, Columbia University, December.

Nelson R. and S. Winters (1982), *An Evolutionary Theory of Economic Change*, Cambridge, MA: Harvard University Press.

Nonaka, I. and H. Takeuchi (1995), *The Knowledge Creating Company*, Oxford: Oxford University Press.

Nuti, F. (1992), *I distretti dell'industria manifatturiera in Italia* (2 volumes), Milan: CNR for Franco Angeli.

OECD (1992), *Technology and the Economy. The Key Relationship*, Paris: OECD.

OECD (1999), *Boosting Innovation: The Cluster Approach*, Paris: OECD.

Ohmae, K. (1990), *The Borderless World: Management Lessons in the New Logic of the Global Market Place*, London: Collins.

Ohmae, K. (1991), *The Borderless World: Power and Strategy in the Interlinked Economy*, New York: Harper and Row.

Paganetto L. and P. Pietrobelli (eds) (2001), *Scienza, Tecnologia e Innovazione: Quali politiche?*, Bologna: Il Mulino.

Park, S. and A. Markusen (1994), 'Generalizing New Industrial Districts: A Theoretical Agenda and an Application from a Non-Western Economy', *Environment and Planning*, A (27).

Park, Y.J. (1998), 'A Comparative Study of Taiwan's and South Korea's SMEs' (in Chinese), Nineteenth Annual Sino-Korean Scholars' Meeting, Taipei, Culture University, 7 August.

Patel, P. and K. Pavitt (1991), 'Large Firms in the Production of the World's Technology: An Important Case of "Non-Globalisation"', *Journal of International Business Studies*, 22, pp. 1-21.

Patrick, H.T. and Y.C. Park (1994), *The Financial Development of Japan, Korea and Taiwan: Growth, Repression and Liberalization*, New York: Oxford University Press.

Penrose, E.T. (1959/1995), *The Theory of the Growth of the Firm*, Oxford: Oxford University Press.

Pietrobelli, C. (1996), *Emerging Forms of Technological Cooperation: The Case for Technology Partnerships – Inner Logic, Examples and Enabling Environment*, Science and Technology Issues, Geneva: UNCTAD.

Pietrobelli, C. (1998), 'The Socio-economic Foundations of Competitiveness: an Econometric Analysis of Italian Industrial Districts', *Industry and Innovation*, 5 (2), pp. 139-55.

Pietrobelli, C. (2000), 'The Role of International Technology Transfer in the Industrialisation of Developing Countries', in M. Elena and D. Schroeer (eds), *Technology Transfer*, Aldershot, UK, Burlington, USA: Ashgate.

Pietrobelli, C. and J. Samper (1997), 'Measurement of Europe-Asia Technology Exchanges: Asymmetry and Distance', *Science and Public Policy*, XXIV (4), August.

Pizzi, P. (1998), 'Il distretto tessile di Teramo', *Economia Marche*, XVII (3), pp. 101-12.

Porter, M. (1990), *The Competitive Advantage of Nations*, London:

Macmillan.

Porter, M. and Ø. Sølvell (1998), 'The Role of Geography in the Process of Innovation and the Sustainable Competitive Advantage of Firms', in A.D. Chandler *et al.* (eds), *The Dynamic Firm. The Role of Technology, Strategy, Organization, and Regions*, Oxford: Oxford University Press.

Pugh, Emerson W. (1984), *Memories that Shaped an Industry. Decision Leading to IBM System/360*, Cambridge, MA: The MIT Press.

Pyke, F., G. Becattini and W. Sengenberger (eds) (1990), *Industrial Districts and Inter-firm Co-operation in Italy*, Geneva: International Institute for Labour Studies.

Pyke, F. and W. Sengenberger (1990), 'Introduction', in F. Pyke, G. Becattini and W. Senbenberger (eds), *Industrial Districts and Inter-firm Co-operation in Italy*, Geneva: International Institute for Labour Studies.

Quirino, P. and G. Rosa (1998), 'Indici di sviluppo delle provincie italiane', *Confindustria, Studi e Documenti*, 7.

Rabellotti, R. (1997), *External Economies and Cooperation in Industrial Districts. A Comparison of Italy and Mexico*, Basingstoke: Macmillan.

Reed Electronics Research (1998), *Yearbook of World Electronics Data*, Volume 2 – America, Japan & Asia Pacific, Sutton, Surrey: Reed Electronics.

Richardson, G.B. (1960/1990), *Information and Investment*, Oxford: Oxford University Press.

Richardson, G.B. (1996), 'Competition, Innovation and Increasing Returns', DRUID Working Paper No. 96-10, July.

Richardson, G.B. (1997), 'Economic Analysis, Public Policy and the Software Industry', DRUID Working Paper No. 97-4, April.

Rugman, A.M. (1997), 'Canada', in J.H. Dunning (ed.), *Governments, Globalization and International Business*, Oxford: Oxford University Press.

San Gee (1990), 'The Status and an Evaluation of the Electronics Industry in Taiwan', OECD Technical Papers No. 29, OECD Development Centre, Paris.

San Gee (1995a), *Technology Support Institutions and Policy Priorities for Industrial Development in Taiwan, R.O.C.*, report prepared for the Ministry of Economic Affairs, Taipei, Taiwan.

San Gee (1995b), 'An Overview of Policy', *Journal of Industry Studies,* 2 (1), pp. 30-42.

San Gee and Wen-jeng Kuo (1998), 'Export Success and Technological Capability: Textiles and Electronics in Taiwan', in D. Ernst, T. Ganiatsos and L. Mytelka (eds), *Technological Capabilities and Export Success – Lessons from East Asia*, London: Routledge.

Santarelli, E., A. Sterlacchini and F. Quaglia (1991), 'Investimenti in macchine e innovazione nelle piccole e medie imprese', *L'Industria*, February, pp. 289-318.

Saxenian, A.L. (1990), 'Regional Networks and the Resurgence of Silicon Valley', *California Management Review*, 33, Fall.

Saxenian, A. (1994), *Regional Advantage: Culture and Competition in Silicon Valley and Route 128*, Cambridge, MA: Harvard University Press.

Saxenian, A. (1999), 'The Silicon Valley-Hsinchu Connection: Technical Communities and Industrial Upgrading', manuscript, Stanford Institute for Economic Policy Research, Stanford University.

Schive, Chi (1990), 'The Next Stage of Industrialization in Taiwan and South Korea', in G. Gereffi and D. Wyman (eds), *Manufacturing Miracles: Paths to Industrialisation in East Asia and Latin America*, Princeton, NJ: Princeton University Press.

Schive, Chi (1993), *Industrial Policies in a Maturing Taiwan Economy*, Taipei: Council for Economic Planning and Development.

Schive, Chi (1995), 'Industrial Policy in a Maturing Taiwan Economy'. *Journal of Industry Studies,* 2 (1), pp. 7-15.

Schmitz, H. and B. Musyck (1994), 'Industrial Districts in Europe: Policy Lessons for Developing Countries?', *World Development*, 22 (6), pp. 889-910.

Schumpeter, J.A. (1934), *The Theory of Economic Development*, Cambridge,

MA: Harvard Economic Studies.

Schumpeter, J.A. (1942), *Capitalism, Socialism, and Democracy*, New York: Harper.

Scitovsky, T. (1990), 'Economic Development in Taiwan and South Korea, 1965-81', in L.J. Lau (ed) *Models of Development. A Comparative Study of Economic Growth in South Korea and Taiwan*, San Francisco: ICS Press.

Scott, A.J. (1998), 'The Geographic Foundations of Industrial Performance', in A.D. Chandler *et al.* (eds), *The Dynamic Firm. The Role of Technology, Strategy, Organization, and Regions*, Oxford: Oxford University Press.

Shieh, G.S. (1990), 'Manufacturing "Bosses": Subcontracting Networks under Dependent Capitalism in Taiwan', dissertation, Department of Sociology, University of California at Berkeley.

Solectron (2000), 'What is a Global Supply-Chain Facilitator?' (www.solectron.com).

Spender, J.-C. (1998), 'The Geographies of Strategic Competence: Borrowing from Social and Educational Psychology to Sketch an Activity and Knowledge-based Theory of the Firm', in A.D. Chandler *et al.* (eds), *The Dynamic Firm. The Role of Technology, Strategy, Organization, and Regions*, Oxford: Oxford University Press.

Stopford, John (1996), 'Implications for National Governments', in John Dunning (ed.), *Globalization, Governments and Competition*, Oxford: Oxford University Press.

Storper, M. and R. Salais (1997), *The Regional World: Territorial Development in the Global Economy*, New York: Guilford Press.

Sturgeon, T. (forthcoming), 'Turnkey Production Networks in Electronics', PhD dissertation, University of California at Berkeley, Department of Urban Planning.

Swann, G.M.P. (1997), 'Towards a Model of Clustering in High-technology Industries', in G.M.P. Swann, M. Prevezer and D. Stout (eds), *The Dynamics of International Clusters: International Comparisons in Computing and Biotechnology*, Oxford and New York: Oxford University Press.

Swann, P., M. Prevezer and D. Stout (eds) (1998), *The Dynamics of Industrial Clustering*, Oxford: Oxford University Press.

Teece, D. (1986), 'Profiting from Technological Innovation', *Research Policy*, 15 (6), pp. 285-306.

Teece, D., G. Pisano and A. Shuen (1997), 'Dynamic Capabilities and Strategic Management', *Strategic Management Journal*, 18, pp. 509-33.

Tray, L.H. (1998), 'A Comparison of Taiwan and South Korea on the Development of SMEs and Economic Policy' (in Chinese), Nineteenth Annual Sino-Korean Scholars' Meeting, Taipei, Culture University, 7 August.

UNCTAD (1995), 'New Technologies and Issues in Technology Capacity Building for Enterprise', mimeograph, Division for Science and Technology, Geneva.

UNCTAD (1998), *World Investment Report 1998. Trends and Determinants*, Geneva: UNCTAD.

United Nations (1995), *World Economic and Social Survey 1995*, New York: United Nations.

Utili, G. (1989), 'Mutamenti organizzativi nei distretti industriali: osservazioni su due casi', in F. Gobbo (ed.), *Distretti e sistemi produttivi alla soglia degli anni '90*, Milan: Franco Angeli.

Viesti, G. (1996), 'Le esportazioni dei principali sistemi produttivi italiani: un'analisi introduttiva', *Rapporto ICE*, Chapter 7.

Viesti, G. (1997), 'Le esportazioni dei sistemi italiani di piccola e media impresa', *ICE, Quaderni di Ricerca*, 3, October.

von Hippel, E. (1988), *The Sources of Innovation*, New York and Oxford: Oxford University Press.

Wade, R. (1990), *Governing the Market: Economic Theory and the Role of Government in East Asian Industrialization*, Princeton, NJ: Princeton University Press.

Walsh, V. (1987), 'Technology, Competitiveness and the Special Problems of Small Countries', *STI Review*, No. 2, Paris: OECD.

Wang, Jiann-Chyuan (1998), 'The Impact of the Asian Financial Crisis on Taiwan's Electronics Firms and Their Possible Responses', mimeo.

Wang, Jiann-Chyuan and Chao-Cheng Mai (1999), 'The Transformation of Industrial Structure and Industrial Development Strategy', *The Economic Development of Taiwan since the 1980s*, Taipei, Taiwan: Chung-Hua Institution for Economic Research.

Williamson, O.E. (1975), *Markets and Hierarchies: Analysis and Antitrust Implications*, New York: The Free Press.

Williamson, O.E. (1985), *The Economic Institutions of Capitalism. Firms, Markets, Relational Contracting*, New York and London: The Free Press.

Wong Poh Kam (1991), *Technological Development through Subcontracting Linkages*, Tokyo: Asia Productivity Organization (APO).

Wong Poh Kam (1995), 'Competing in the Global Electronics Industry: A Comparative Analysis of the Strategy of Taiwan and Singapore', paper presented at the international conference on 'The Experience of Industrial Development in Taiwan', National Central University, Taiwan, May.

Wu, H.L. and T.C. Chou (1990), 'Taiwan's Industrial Structural Transformation and De-Industrialization', *Industry of Free China*, 74 (4), pp. 11-25.

Wu, Se-Hwa and Liu Hwei-Lu (1996), 'A Study on the Dynamic Network Organizational-Type in the High Technology Industry' (in Chinese), Conference on Technology and Industrial Networks, Taipei, National Cheng-Chi University, 25 September.

Wu, Se-Hwa and Shen Jung-Chin (1998), 'Network-Type and Network Governance: The Taiwanese Experience', Seventeenth Strategic Management Society Annual International Conference, Barcelona, 5-8 October.

Zander, U. and B. Kogut (1995), 'Knowledge and the Speed of the Transfer and Imitation of Organizational Capabilities: An Empirical Test', *Organizational Science*, 6 (1).

Annex 1: Questionnaires: Garments Sector and Electronics Sector

QUESTIONNAIRE: GARMENTS SECTOR

A. Company Background

1. Company name...

2. Year of establishment...

3. Location/city...

4. Number of plants/sites..

5. Company status (please tick as many as apply)

a. Independent	
b. Subsidiary	
c. Stock market quoted	
d. Foreign owned (please give % foreign ownership)	%

6. Total employees (average full-time equivalents in each year)

1995	
1996	
1997	

7. Gross value of plant and equipment (current book value) ....

8. Total sales (value of sales) for last three years

1995	
1996	
1997	

9.   Value of exports for last three years (in local currency or US dollars)

1995	
1996	
1997	

10. Percentage of exports to:

Region	Last year	3 years ago
a. European Union countries		
b. European countries: non-EU member states		
c. North America		
d. Asia		
e. Rest of the world		
Total	100%	100%

11. a. R&D expenditure last year (1997)…………………………………...
     b. Total number of employees in R&D
        (full-time equivalents)………………………………………………….
     c. Total number of university-trained scientists and engineers in R&D
        (full-time equivalents)……………………………………………….

12.   What are your company's main products?

	Last year	3 years ago
a.		
b.		
c.		
d.		
e.		

13. a. Give the average number of customers of your firm last year   (1997)
        …………………………………………………………………………
     b. What percentage of your output is currently sold to your top 3
        customers?………….. %
     c. Which is the main economic sector they belong to?…………………...

B. Background of Entrepreneur/Founder

14. Does the founder of the firm have a university degree?
    (please tick all that apply)

a. No	
b. Yes – Business management / finance	
c. Yes – Science/engineering	
d. Yes – Other	

15. How important, for the operation of the current enterprise, was the founder's previous work experience in the following categories? (10 = very important; 1 = unimportant: please insert appropriate numbers)

	Local	*Abroad*
a. Family business		
b. Small and medium-sized enterprise		
c. Large national firm		
d. Multinational firm		
e. University		
f. Government laboratory		
g. Research institute		

C. Other Performance Indicators

16. What was your ratio of pre-tax profit to sales in the last 3 years?

1995	
1996	
1997	

17. Has your firm introduced or adopted any major innovations in products, processes or the organization of production during the last three years? (please tick the relevant boxes and describe very briefly)

	No	Yes	**IF YES, were these innovations already in use in:**			
			Your Industry	Other industries	Not in use by anyone else	Do not know
Major changes To products?						

Describe:

	No	Yes	Your Industry	Other industries	Not in use by anyone else	Do not know
Major changes to processes?						

Describe:

	No	Yes	Your Industry	Other industries	Not in use by anyone else	Do not know
Major changes to the organization of production?						

Describe:

18. What sales were generated from new products launched in the last year (1997) (excluding minor modifications to existing products)?...............

19. Regarding your main product (please tick all that apply)

a. the distributor can sell competing products to yours	
b. you can sell via other distributors	

20. How many technology licences have you sold?

    a. To national firms..................
    b. To international firms............

21. How many technology licenses have you purchased?

    a. From national firms..................
    b. From international firms............

22. How many patents does your firm have?...............

23. Do you have strategic partnerships with global technological/market leaders involving substantial joint efforts that go beyond standard agreements for product development? ....Yes/No

24. Is your firm IS0-9000 accredited? ....Yes/No

D. Skills and Employee Remuneration

25. Skilled employees

	Current	*3 years ago*
Number of university scientists & engineers		
Number of technicians holding diplomas		

26. What is the annual salary paid to:

	Newly recruited	*5 years experience*
University trained staff		
Staff with diploma		
Shop floor worker		

27. What is your average labour turnover rate per year?
(number of newly recruited/total number of employees) ....(%)

E. Sources of Technology

28. How important are the following as sources of technical knowledge for your firm? (10 = very important; 1 = unimportant: please insert appropriate numbers)

Sources internal to the firm

Formal R&D performed in house	
Other in-house technological activities	

External sources

	Local	National	International
Recruitment			
Customers			
Equipment suppliers			
Other suppliers			
Licensing			
Horizontal partnerships (with firms Producing similar products): - Formal partnerships - Informal interactions			
Industry associations			
Universities			
Public research or design institutions			
Consultants			
Government extension services			
Trade fairs			
Publications			

F. Process Capabilities

29. What was your ratio of value of end-of-year inventory to sales?

Last year	3 years ago

30. What is your average order-to-delivery time?

Current	3 years ago

31. What is the reject rate for your products?

Current	3 years ago

32. How has the unit cost of production (in real terms) for your main product changed over the last three years? (please tick one)

Remained the same	
Fallen by 1-10%	
Fallen by more than 10%	
Increased	

33. If unit cost in the last question has fallen, how important as a cause have been improvements that your company has made to process technologies in your company, including machinery (but excluding purchases of new process technologies and machinery)? (please tick one)

Very important	
Rather important	
Unimportant	

G. Training

34. Expenditure on training last year (1997)..........

35. Percentage spent on training from external sources.......... %

H. Clustering Effects

36. a. What percentage of last year's (1997) output went to ......?

	Local	*National*	*International*	
1. Physical output markets				100%
2. Service markets				100%

b. What percentage of last year's (1997) input came from......?

	Local	National	International	
1. Physical input markets:				
a. raw materials and				
components				100%
b. capital goods & equipment				100%
2. Service input markets				100%
3. Skilled labour markets				100%
4. Finance				100%

37. How intense/frequent is your firm's interaction with the following *local* institutions/organisations? (10 = very important; 1 = unimportant: please insert appropriate numbers)

	Local	National	International
1. Customers			
2. Suppliers			
3. Competitors			
4. Financial institutions:			
- public			
- private			
5. Service providers			
6. Government agencies			
7. Government laboratories			
8. Industry associations			
9. Training institutions:			
- public			
- private			
10. Universities			

I. Respondent's Details

38. Respondent's name...

39. Respondent's position in firm..

40. Respondent's address...

41. Respondent's phone number..

42. Respondent's fax number..

43. Respondent's e-mail address...

QUESTIONNAIRE: ELECTRONICS SECTOR

A. Company Background

1. Company name..

2. Year of establishment....................

3. Location/city..

4. Number of plants/sites...............................

5. Company status (please tick as many as apply)

a. Independent	
b. Subsidiary	
c. Stock market quoted	
d. Foreign owned (please give % foreign ownership)	%

6. Total employees (average full-time equivalents in each year)

1995	
1996	
1997	

7. Gross value of plant and equipment (current book value) ....

8. Total sales (value of sales) for last three years

1995	
1996	
1997	

9.   Value of exports for last three years (in local currency or US dollars)

1995	
1996	
1997	

10. Percentage of exports to:

Region	Last year	3 years ago
a. European Union countries		
b. European countries: non-EU member states		
c. North America		
d. Asia		
e. Rest of the world		
Total	100%	100%

11. a. R&D expenditure last year (1997)..............................
     b. Total number of employees in R&D (full-time equivalents)..............
     c. Total number of university-trained scientists and engineers in R&D
        (full-time equivalents)...................

12. What are your company's three main products?

	Last year	3 years ago
a.		
b.		
c.		

13. a. Give the average number of customers of your firm last year (1997)....
     b. What percentage of your output is currently sold to your top 3
        customers?.......... %
     c. Which is the main economic sector they belong to?......................

B. Background of Entrepreneur/Founder

14. Does the founder of the firm have a University degree?
    (please tick all that apply)

a. No	
b. Yes – Business management / finance	
c. Yes – Science/engineering	
d. Yes – Other	

15. How important, for the operation of the current enterprise, was the founder's previous work experience in the following categories? (10 = very important; 1 = unimportant: please insert appropriate numbers):

	Local	*Abroad*
a. Family business		
b. Small and medium-sized enterprise		
c. Large national firm		
d. Multinational firm		
e. University		
f. Government laboratory		
g. Research institute		

C. Other Performance Indicators

16. What was your ratio of pre-tax profit to sales in the last 3 years?

1995	
1996	
1997	

17. Has your firm introduced or adopted any major innovations in products, processes or the organisation of production during the last three years? (please tick the relevant boxes and describe very briefly)

	No	Yes	**IF YES, were these innovations already in use in:**			
			Your industry	Other industries	Not in use by anyone else	Do not Know
Major changes to products?						

Describe:

Major changes to processes?						

Describe:

Major changes to the organization of production?						

Describe:

18. What sales were generated from new products launched in the last year (1997) (excluding minor modifications to existing products)?..............

19. Do you have distribution contracts with market leaders/major distributors? (please tick one)

a. No	
b. Yes – non-exclusive contract(s)	
c. Yes – and the distributor cannot distribute competing products	

20. How many technology licences have you sold?

    a. To national firms...
    b. To international firms......................................

21. How many technology licences have you purchased?

    a. From national firms.......................................
    b. From international firms.................................

22. How many patents does your firm have?...............

23. Do you have strategic partnerships with global technological/market leaders involving substantial joint efforts that go beyond standard agreements for product development?..............Yes/No

24. Is your firm IS0-9000 accredited?...............Yes/No

D. Capital Market Performance For Stock Market Listed Firms

25. Please calculate your Index of Return on Investments

Market value at Initial Public Offering (IPO) .... = ...
Total funds invested up to IPO*

* Total funds invested up to IPO = Shareholder Equity – Funds raised from IPO + Cumulative losses (or – Profit) (at date of IPO or of Acquisition)

E. Skills and Employee Remuneration

26. Skilled employees

	Current	*3 years ago*
Number of university scientists & engineers		
Number of technicians holding diplomas		

27. What is the annual salary paid to:

	Newly recruited	*5 years experience*
University trained staff		
Staff with diploma		
Shop floor worker		

28. What is your average labour turn over rate per year?
     (number of newly recruited/total number of employees)..............(%)

F. Sources of Technology

29. How important are the following as sources of technical knowledge for your firm? (10 = very important; 1 = unimportant: please insert appropriate numbers)

Sources internal to the firm

Formal R&D performed in house	
Other in-house technological activities	

External sources

	Local	National	International
Recruitment			
Customers			
Equipment suppliers			
Other suppliers			
Licensing			
Horizontal partnerships (with firms producing similar products): - Formal partnerships - Informal interactions			
Industry associations			
Universities			
Public research or design institutions			
Consultants			
Government extension services			
Trade fairs			
Publications			

G. Process Capabilities

30. What was your ratio of value of end-of-year inventory to sales?

Last Year	3 years ago

31. What is your average order-to-delivery time?

Current	3 years ago

32. What is the reject rate for your products?

Current	3 years ago

33. How has the unit cost of production (in real terms) for your main product changed over the last three years? (please tick one)

Remained the same	
Fallen by 1-10%	
Fallen by more than 10%	
Increased	

34. If unit cost in the last question has fallen, how important as a cause have been improvements that your company has made to process technologies in your company, including machinery (but excluding purchases of new process technologies and machinery)? (please tick one)

Very important	
Rather important	
Unimportant	

H. Training

35. Expenditure on training last year (1997)..........

36. Percentage spent on training from external sources.......... %

I. Clustering Effects

37. a. What percentage of last year's (1997) output went to ......?

	Local	National	International	
1. Physical output markets				100%
2. Service markets				100%

b. What percentage of last year's (1997) input came from......?

	Local	National	International	
1. Physical input markets: a. raw materials and components				100%
b. capital goods & equipment				100%
2. Service input markets				100%
3. Skilled labour markets				100%
4. Finance				100%

38. How intense/frequent is your firm's interaction with the following *local* institutions/organizations? (10 = very important; 1 = unimportant: please insert appropriate numbers)

	Local	*National*	*International*
1. Customers			
2. Suppliers			
3. Competitors			
4. Financial institutions: - public - private			
5. Service providers			
6. Government agencies			
7. Government laboratories			
8. Industry associations			
9. Training institutions: - public - private			
10. Universities			

J. Respondent's Details

39. Respondent's name..

40. Respondent's position in firm..

41. Respondent's address...

42. Respondent's phone number..

43. Respondent's fax number...

44. Respondent's e-mail address...

Index